PRAISE FOR *THIS IS HOW A ROBIN DRINKS*

"Smart, funny, and shot through with aching love, *This Is How a Robin Drinks* is both a call to action and a balm for the solastalgic heart. This profoundly beautiful, desperately necessary book will change how you see the world and every living thing within it, including yourself."
 —MARGARET RENKL, author of *The Comfort of Crows: A Backyard Year*

"Inspiring and full of wonder. These vivid stories combine curiosity, wit, and a keen sense of the many ways that exultation and heartbreak mingle when we look closely at the everyday life of our yards, parks, and cities."
 —DAVID GEORGE HASKELL, author of *Sounds Wild and Broken: Sonic Marvels, Evolution's Creativity, and the Crisis of Sensory Extinction*

"Joanna Brichetto is a suburban Thoreau. In fifty-three crisp essays that can be read as daily meditation, she takes us to pocket parks, dead mall parking lots, and concrete canyons in pursuit of little ecological marvels. This collection is essential to understanding the need for widespread habitat protection and restoration and a reminder of the capacity and limits of nature to resist human destruction."
 —GEORGANN EUBANKS, author of *Saving the Wild South: The Fight for Native Plants on the Brink of Extinction*

"It would be hard to imagine a more delightful, engaging, and insightful introduction to urban natural history. Brichetto's love of nature is infectious, and with a little luck it will go viral and infect us all. Her laugh-out-loud wittiness draws us in for more and reminds us to hit the pause button on our hectic lives as an antidote to the day's news."

 —DOUGLAS W. TALLAMY, author of *Nature's Best Hope: A New Approach to Conservation That Starts in Your Yard*

THIS IS HOW A ROBIN DRINKS

THIS IS HOW
a
ROBIN DRINKS

Essays on Urban Nature

JOANNA BRICHETTO

TERRA FIRMA BOOKS | TRINITY UNIVERSITY PRESS | SAN ANTONIO

Published by Terra Firma Books, an imprint of
Trinity University Press
San Antonio, Texas 78212

Book design by BookMatters
Cover design by Anne Richmond Boston
Author photo by Maggie Rose
Cover art: iStock/Summer Heat/Tomacco,
iStock/Nest/jordifa, AdobeStock/Bird/mtruchon

Image captions: frontis, Centennial Sportsplex, Nashville, late winter, American
field pansy with sycamore seeds in a parking lot crack; summer, old clothes,
new Gulf fritillary hanging out to dry; fall, American sycamore leaves on sewer
cover, Twenty-Sixth Avenue South, Nashville; winter, ring-billed gulls at the
corner of Nolensville Road and Harding Place, Nashville; spring, catalpa tree
flowers from sidewalks at Vanderbilt University

ISBN 978-1-59534-299-7 paper
ISBN 978-1-59534-300-0 ebook

Trinity University Press strives to produce its books using methods and materials in an environmentally sensitive manner. We favor working with manufac-
turers that practice sustainable management of all natural resources, produce
paper using recycled stock, and manage forests with the best possible practices
for people, biodiversity, and sustainability. The press is a member of the Green
Press Initiative, a nonprofit program dedicated to supporting publishers in
their efforts to reduce their impacts on endangered forests, climate change, and
forest-dependent communities.

CIP data on file at the Library of Congress

28   27   26   25   24 | 5   4   3   2

For Michael, Maggie, and Izzy

Contents

Preface

This Is How a Robin Drinks: Essays on Urban Nature offers a new version of several old hunches: that by paying attention to the natural world we have a chance to figure out who, where, and when we are; that by getting to know the living beings around us, we come to a more sustainable vision of our place among them; that the more particular a story, the more universal; that suffering is inexplicable and unredeemable but strangely useful to the imagination; and that nature is all around.

"Urban nature" is a complex and inadequate term for a complex and inadequate habitat. We make more every day. We pave paradise as quick as we can, and even redevelop developed land, where infill—in the name of density—makes scarce the creatures who had been able to eke out a living. These are things we need to see clearly if we are to meddle productively.

Seeing clearly is how I "make shift with things as they are," like Aldo Leopold in *Sand County Almanac.* But who am I? Leopold was the father of wildlife ecology who spent weekends in a cabin on degraded land, where he got his "meat from God." I'm the mother of two who lives by a sidewalk on degraded land, where I get my tofu from Trader Joe's. But like Leopold, I cannot live without wild things.

This is my almanac: sketches arranged by season, set in the backyard, the sidewalk, the park, the parking lot, connected by urgent wonder. Not just the gobsmacked astonishment kind of wonder, but wonder as in to ponder, to question. Both kinds of wonder lead to connect, which leads to love, which leads to protect. We can't protect what we don't love, and we can't love what we haven't met, and we can't meet what is always someplace else, where many of us think nature stays.

Nature is right outside our door, and here's what I've learned: nature is the door too, and what's on the inside. Nature is the jumping spider on the screen, the assassin bug in the shower, the ladybug at the lamp. Nature is moss on brick where gutters spill, a sycamore sprout in the storm drain. It's a blue jay; it's bur oak. Nature is a full moon over the electric substation, as viewed from a bridge on the interstate. It's red ants in the mailbox, a redtail on the steeple, and pretty much everything at the next red light. Nature is under our feet, over our head, and beside us—the very places we need to know first.

So let's look around. Time is short. And none of us can live without wild things.

Some unwonted, taught pride diverts us

from our original intent, which is to explore

the neighborhood, view the landscape, to

discover at least where it is that we have been

so startlingly set down, if we can't learn why.

ANNIE DILLARD
Pilgrim at Tinker Creek

Summer

Vocation

In fourth grade I narrowed it to three: detective, librarian, naturalist. "Naturalist" explained why I spent all my free time in the yard or under trees, down the bat cave, or where the cow bones floated ashore.

But then puberty happened. I got distracted. And then *blah, blah*, the usual story: I forgot what I loved; I lost myself in a boy, and had I been a better detective I never would have married him. To my credit, I did find a job in a library.

For maybe fifteen years I didn't wych my way to the nearest water or any water. Bugs were for killing. I didn't hear birds, didn't bring home a single leaf, didn't pocket acorns. Not even one sweet hickory, and those are good eats by any standard.

Then I found a man in that library, and although this too is the usual story, our version bore inspection. It checked out. And I remembered.

The first clue—the clanging moment I knew my fourth-grade self was climbing her way back in—was when the man and I were on a walk and I pointed past the streetlight and spoke aloud a thing that surfaced as true and welcome as yellow cow bones in water weeds. It might have been a prayer, or a poem. It was this: "Before I met you, that was a bird in a tree. Now it's a blue jay in a hackberry."

And this explains why I spend all my free time in the yard and under trees, looking around: investigating, cataloging, memorizing what and who are in the wide world with me. Because I narrowed it to one.

Dragonfly, Secondhand

At Goodwill last August, a thing flew past my face. I was near the however-many-toys-you-can-cram-in-a-bag-for-$2.99 table, which is where one might expect to meet projectiles, but the thing was not a Hot Wheels car or Nerf bullet. It was alive. And I was the only one who saw.

It perched on a T-shirt.

Goodwill tends to sort clothes by color, especially T-shirts. The men's T-shirt section is a vision of order. Only if hung in rainbow sequence could it be more beautiful. The flying thing aimed for the well-represented whites of the T-shirt spectrum. Right there on a shoulder seam: a dragonfly. Gorgeous. White body with black-striped wings in perch position: all four straight out and still. I kept still, too. When a shopper wheeled close, the dragonfly flew and I followed.

It perched on a ball cap.

Let me describe another merchandising tactic at which our Goodwill excels: ball caps. Above the highest wall rack around the perimeter of the store is a frieze of finishing nails. That many nails are necessary to accommodate donated caps because this is Nashville, and who doesn't have at least five caps at home and two in the car? I don't mean caps for ball games, although there will be some, but caps for every day: trucker hats. Mesh in back with snap closure, poly-cotton billboard in front with a logo. They are taller than athletic caps. Plenty of room for a dragonfly.

This dragonfly had found a white cap. It paused. I paused. Were those wing stripes more brown than black? Hard to tell under fluorescent lights.

Here I fretted someone would notice me acting weird, someone would notice the dragonfly, and someone would smack the dragonfly with secondhand sporting-goods equipment. But I was helpless to the chase. I tried to chase more casually.

Next it flew to color-coded ladies' short-sleeved sweaters and found another white shoulder. Then back to the white cap. What was up with all the white?

Not that color was my only question. Why was there a dragonfly in Goodwill? What kind was it? How could a dragonfly get out of Goodwill? How could I help a dragonfly get out of Goodwill?

I already knew that every day, dragonflies throughout the world are losing habitat. I knew that in our own neighborhood the one storm sewer with a prayer of supporting semiaquatic life got drained years ago. We found a baby snapping turtle there once, and another time—directly under a streetlamp—we watched an orange salamander toddle across a driveway. This was when we still had puddles, before "grade improvements." After the grading, no wildlife, but SUVs in the driveway keep their tires clean.

One of my Goodwill questions was answered later, with a field guide: common whitetail (*Plathemis lydia*), male. Known for perching on mud or on anything at all, known for basking in sun. Females lay eggs in shallow ponds after mating with the male, which patrols the favored spot. Adults eat flying insects, can fly far from water, and do not live long—maybe a month, maybe more.

There is no mud or sun at Goodwill. There is no water, unless one counts the Scary Bathroom We Never Use. There is no prey but the odd moth or mosquito. There are only shoppers hunting for bargains.

If my family is wearing clothes (and we usually are), the clothes came from Goodwill (or Target), period. My clothes are even thriftier: they come from my kids' hand-me-ups, which came from Goodwill (or Target). I get classroom materials at Goodwill. I get soccer cleats. I get housewares, books, bedding, toys, office supplies. Once there was a pair of rubber hip waders flopped all by their lonesome on top of men's dress shirts, and had they been remotely close to my size I would have bought them so fast my wallet would have been the flying projectile that day. Which goes to show that, though thrifty, I am not immune to impulse.

Impulse must explain why the dragonfly flew in. The shop is part of a busy city grid, but the two glass doors face a railway easement across the street: a mini wasteland of exotic thistle, bindweed, johnsongrass, and whatever else can survive railroad herbicides. Maybe those weeds looked like home. Maybe those double doors—so shiny when they open and close, open and close—maybe they shimmered

like water. Maybe the male was on the hunt for new terri-
tory to patrol. And once he made it through the waterfall
(double-glazed glass), he basked on pale mud (T-shirt, cap,
sweater) to get his bearings.

When the dragonfly perched again on the white cap, I
eased a neighboring cap off a nail and sidled toward him. I
don't remember being self-conscious at that moment. I was
predator, he was prey, and we were all that was. My trucker
hat ate him in one go, and with my other hand I swooped
his ball cap under and in. I racewalked toward the door but
detoured to the cashier nearest it to gush, I hoped intelligi-
bly, "I've captured a dragonfly in these hats and I'm going
to set it free outside and I'll be right back." Because at this
point, with my prey caught, we were no longer all that was,
and I felt I had to explain why I was leaving the store with
two hats I did not stand in line to pay for. The lady raised her
chin as an "Okay, whatever."

The waterfall parted with a push of my hip, and I stopped
at the edge of the concrete porch. I faced the easement and
the sun. I straightened my arms and lifted the trucker hat
from the white one. The dragonfly shot toward the little
field, away, completely. Gone.

I wanted to look for him, to scan the railroad weeds for
a pond or even a puddle, to see that he stayed completely
gone, but I was too nervous about stolen merchandise so I
turned around.

The doors looked like doors.

I had a smile ready for the cashier when I would tell her
"It was fine, the dragonfly was free," and "thanks," but she

didn't look up so I didn't say it. In that crowded store, I was still the only person to see the dragonfly.

What if I hadn't been there? What would have happened? If a dragonfly falls in Goodwill and no one is there to hear it, does it make a sound?

Slow now, and tired, I stepped past customers and children and carts to loop back to the frieze, to hook the hats on their respective nails. And then I perched. To get my bearings. I stood in an aisle—any aisle, I can't remember which—and basked in fluorescence, trying to think what I'd come to Goodwill for in the first place.

Naked Ladies and Cicadas

Whoever planted our surprise lilies is gone, but her lilies aren't. For twenty-three Nashville summers they've surprised us in the front yard: pink megaphones on a stick. Hummingbirds love them, but I didn't until now. Other names for the plant are resurrection lilies, which my family is too Jewish to say; and naked ladies, which we think is funny. They *are* nekkid. The leaves that ought to clothe them come and go in spring, months before fleshy flower stalks stretch.

I must have asked my neighbor what they were. Mrs. Neal liked to chat from her porch as she flung Lean Cuisine leftovers onto the grass ("for the birds"). She had been at the house next door for forty years. She would have known the name naked lady, and would have cackled when she said it.

Ours surprised me two days ago. I forgot them, as usual, until pink unfolded.

A cicada found that first bloom a day later. As I bent to stick my nose in the flower I saw an empty skin clutching the lowest petal. It was a big annual dog-day cicada. And at that moment, as I squinted over my glasses in search of the curly white thread inside a cicada's split back—part of its breathing apparatus—right then, morning sun shot through it. The husk was a conduit. Sunshine poured through the eye bubbles, sluiced from the front claws, pricked each chin whisker, and lit the whole miraculous thing on fire. What had been dry-mud-brown burned amber, burned my eyes. It was so gorgeous I could not move except to toggle myself toward the best angle of sun through skin.

Exuvia is the proper word: "the cast-off outer skin of an arthropod after a molt." Exuuuuuuvia. An exuvia exalted.

The nymph had tunneled during the moon-thin night, up through soil soft from a storm, and scaled the first vertical thing it met: a naked lady. When it reached the top, it stopped on a petal to do its own disrobing. Scratches show where clawed feet scrabbled for a hold. Cicadas, like butterflies, have to hang just so to give new wings space and gravity to straighten, fill, and firm. *Surprise*: a nekkid bug, resurrected.

Does anyone plant surprise lilies anymore? *Lycoris squamigera* is an old flower in old lawns. In our neighborhood they still show up, but only in yards not yet gentrified by sod. They thrive on neglect and will not survive weekly mow 'n' blow yard crews. My family is lazy, so we are ideal hosts.

Our fallow yard is good for cicadas too. They spend most of their lives underground sucking roots, not doing any harm. Depending on species, they'll stay two to seventeen years in the dark, then emerge to molt into adults: to fly, sing (if male), mate, lay eggs (if female), and a few weeks later, die.

I worry about the collateral damage new construction wreaks on cicada populations. Nashville is booming. We are a city of cranes. Excavation kills cicadas outright, but my Twilight Zone nightmare is an image of Nashville's thirteen-year periodical nymphs tunneling to the surface to find no surface. Instead they bump whiskered chins against new infill houses planted two per lot, against zero-setback additions and new mixed-use high-rises: obstacles so deep and wide any bug left alive would not feel its way to an edge in time.

After Mrs. Neal left, six successive owners renovated, landscaped, flipped, and otherwise "improved" her property. The side porch where she welcomed us to the neighborhood with buttermilk pie is behind a six-foot privacy fence. Surprise lilies (deliberately) and cicadas (incidentally) were grubbed out years ago.

Yesterday's cicada was male. Where is he now? Did he stay? Is he part of the buzzing chorus in the hackberry trees, singing his chainsaw booty call for any female within cicada earshot?

Males start calling as the day warms. They sing and sing from tymbal tums, some with vibrato, some tremolo. Vibrato changes pitch, but tremolo—like a guitar pedal, like a Purim gragger—stays the pitch but pulses it. Sometimes a cicada waves a pattern in 2/4 time: the downbeat a ratcheting socket wrench, the upbeat a rest. They all crescendo, quicken, fade, repeat.

At dusk they quiet. Except one, maybe, and maybe he's mine: my naked lady cicada. He stays up late to solo in trees already black, even as robins *tut tut* last call from tonight's roost. And if dark comes early because of cloud cover, fooling the rest of us, he will sing even as big brown bats start their turn in pewter sky. He will sing with the moon, but I have his skin, which once held the sun.

Walking Onions

Walking onions walk. Mom, never one to visit empty-handed, showed up with a muddy bouquet in a sack unasked for, unexplained. I liked the name. By the next year, or the next, or maybe the one after that, my garden had little else.

They walk by gravity. A green strap spears up—tall, more than halfway up the chicken wire—and the tip swells into a manila paper bunting of babies: bulblets with spears-in-waiting tiny as pine needles. The needles grow, bulblets fatten, and the collective family leans, creases, and pivots to the ground. The babies root a foot or more from where they started or tumble even farther. They walk, true to name. They take a step, and another, and so on across the garden into the grass.

Chicken wire is no barrier to a peripatetic vegetable.

They crowded the parsley, the chives, the basil, even the chickweed and ground ivy, but at least I was growing something. And besides, they were from Mom.

They gave me a surprise, those onions, because of the paper wasps. One summer I kept hearing something: a dry scratchy something. Curiosity finally pulled me from the hammock to the garden. To the walking onions. To the paper wasp on the paper of the walking onions. The wasp did not mind my giant face stuck up in her business of scraping paper. I could see jaws working the fiber, planing it top to bottom, not side to side; tucking it in a hidden cheek to fly back to the nest where she would spit a new wall, slobber a tight hexagonal nursery.

Paper wasps were the only things that chewed those onions. They did not taste good raw, fried, marinated, grilled, souped, chived, baked, or roasted.

I finally mentioned this to Mom.

She said that's why she got rid of hers in the first place.

And, apparently, why she walked them to me.

Paradise in a Parking Lot

I like it when a flower or a little tuft of grass
grows through a crack in the concrete.
It's so f--kin' heroic.

GEORGE CARLIN

In summer twilight before dawn, Orion the Hunter wakes up here, in the vacant lot. Fresh from the horizon, he's lying on his back, but his bow is aimed at the Bull who with every ticking moment pulls him upright and west. The Bull's route is the ecliptic, the same route the moon takes, and the sun, and the zodiac signs; and which I learned from a book but took on faith until the vacant lot's lesson. There is more sky here than at home.

The path arcs above the parking spaces where my son Izzy learned to ride a bike, circling round and round the building's empty footprint where his sister Maggie learned twelve years before, when the footprint was full. It arcs above the busy street beyond, above new condos, above the tutoring center that keeps classrooms bright all night behind walls of glass. It gets poked by the cell tower where crows sit and talk while the sky fades, after they've chased the hawk from the hackberry.

This lot pulls me through the neighborhood like the Bull

pulls the Hunter. I hunt for marvels that tolerate intolerable conditions: nostoc at the elevator shaft, moss on what's left of the lobby, asters in cracks. In the corner where skateboarders built a ramp and brought in a broken armoire to jump over grows a baby sugarberry no one has bothered to kill, and for two summers it has been the only place I've seen a convergent ladybug: a native beetle with two charming white marks on the thorax, the bit between head and wings. The marks slant toward each other—think emoji eyebrows, or a backslash and a forward slash—and if, as in geometry class, you imagine that those lines continue, they would converge. Thus, convergent.

If I'm too late for stars, I'm on time for morning glories. This is the vine that every year remembers to twine through the chain-link. Weed eaters can't touch it, because seeds fall on the wild side, next to a twenty-foot drop. I watch from the tame side, at eye level.

When a bee dives into a blue trumpet, all I see is her fuzzy black butt speckled with pollen and two back legs braced wide, with feet shaped like tiny ship's anchors. Her butt shivers while her front is busy with the bloom's white throat, but she doesn't buzz. Not until four seconds later, when she backs out, swivels, then buzzes to the next blue trumpet. I hear humming from six matching bees: the common eastern bumble bees I wish were more common. There are forty flowers. Each bloom lives one day. Each bumblebee lives one month, maybe two.

Adjacent landscapes don't have bees, because their lawns are just grass and their flowers are just for people. Typical bedding annuals track the seasons but feed no one: winter's pansies are replaced by spring's begonias are replaced by fall's mums. And when redevelopment replaces old hardwoods with crape myrtles, the trees aren't food either.

But at the vacant lot wild fencerow trees help make up the deficit. Black cherry, redbud, sugar maple, walnut, black oak. And then there's the sentinel tree: one magnificent hackberry, open-grown in full sun because it is surrounded by cement. The leaves are food for insects that feed warblers all year, and the berries keep our robins alive in winter. Any street-side hackberry this big and healthy is paradise.

If you are a Joni Mitchell fan, you know where I'm going with this. Joni sings, grieving in a happy key, "Don't it always seem to go, that you don't know what you've got till it's gone? They paved paradise and put up a parking lot." But what if paradise is *in* a parking lot? I know what I've got till it's gone. I walk this lot every day and will do so until the property owners win the zoning change that will turn one and half acres of asphalt into one and half acres of mixed-use high-rise.

My husband, Michael, warns that if I run around calling parking lots paradise, people will misunderstand. They'll assume I don't believe in land protections, or that I value a built environment over a natural one, or that I don't realize our world is burning quicker than we can put out the fire.

Our world is beautiful as it burns.

"Your view is fragile," he worries. "You want people to look around and see how resilient and wonderful nature is, even in degraded places. You think this will make them protect all of nature."

"True."

"Imagine what a normal person would think if you say this is paradise." He waves at the rubble. "They'd say, 'Look, here's grass in a crack! Nature is fine! Let's make more parking lots!'"

"But this lot is special. It's neglected. It lets life back in."

"So there's good lots and bad lots?"

Four blocks away is another corner lot, but smaller and not vacant. It's "maintained." An unrelieved sea of pavement runs from sidewalk to sidewalk and is pressure washed so dirt can't settle. The only plants are a row of Chinese elm in the hellstrip, the sliver of lawn between sidewalk and street. Nothing local can eat those leaves. When the leaves fall, nothing can use them as cover, because they are blown into bags right away. *Cleanliness is next to godliness*, says this church lot, but I feel certain the church's god would prefer to maintain Creation rather than prevent it.

At the vacant lot's no trespassing sign, look down. Along with the usual turfgrass from other continents, the lawn is made of little barley, nimblewill, sedges, and white grass, all native. And here are blue violets, yellow sorrel, Carolina cranesbill, buttercup, field pansy, and "naturalized" wildflowers like white clover, hop trefoil, chickweed, vetch, dead nettle, speedwell, henbit, and the tiny purple stars of field madder. Last year I found a bank of white crosses—each the size of a button on a shirt cuff—and met my first Virginia buttonweed.

The slope that gave little Maggie and Izzy thrills on their bikes is now a silted floodplain the length of a school bus. Butterweed finds it. The rosettes star the mud for months, then raise fat fleshy stems that burst into bouquets of yellow flowers brighter than butter.

This year I found two clumps of a mystery bunchgrass. As they grew taller, they drained from green to tan, and when tufty blooms jutted zig zag up the stem, the phrase "bird-of-paradise" kept flying into my head. That's the name of a tropical flower with a horizontal "beak" of petals, which does resemble, in a fancy way, my humble grass. But all native bunchgrass is paradise for groundbirds. They need it for cover, food, and nesting.

On a hunch, I checked my notes and found a hike at Flat Rock where a botanist showed us *Andropogon virginicus*, or broom sedge. My notes were meant to help me identify grasses in the wild, and it was his phrase that flew to me in the wild of my city lot: "This one," he said, "looks like bird-of-paradise."

But even I know this parking lot isn't paradise. If it were, it wouldn't be a parking lot. It would be a pocket park I make with my millions of dollars. I'd work with conservation partners and neighborhood volunteers to de-pave it; plant it in local genotype, straight species flowers, shrubs, and trees; install walkways; build benches, arbors, and a bird blind; and craft the corner down by the storm drain into a pond big enough for bats to swoop through for drinks. We'd have a demo patch of bare earth for the mining bees— and for birds to dust bathe and butterflies to puddle. A bat house, purple martin gourds, a tower for chimney swifts. It would be a certified Monarch Waystation, a warbler mecca. Brush pile, compost, nature play, rain barrels. There'd be a labeled teaching garden of all the native plants that just happen when lawns don't get treated with herbicides, so neighbors could recognize them at home. And a tiny garden of the invasives that also happen, so neighbors could learn those too. There'd be interpretive signs made by local artists, a picture-book story trail. Let's add a mini amphitheater for events, some picnic tables, and a long-ass wall that gives Twenty-First Avenue South a glorious crowd-sourced mural of the plant and animal players in our local watershed, from limestone bedrock on up, from springtails to red-tails.

"Don't let go of the fence!" I yell, instead of "Don't die." It's nearly lunchtime, and Izzy and Michael and I are in the lot to walk Beatrice, who is right now chasing sticks. But Izzy is twenty feet above me, sidling atop the broken wall at the wild side of the morning glories. His back is to the chainlink, his front faces the drop, and his feet are longer than the ledge they balance on.

Michael, unconcerned, hurls another stick. Izzy, uncon-cerned, takes another step.

Right then a shrill whistling pulls me to two hawks over-head, directly above Izzy but higher than the cell tower. They wheel slowly, one above the other in hot blue sky, and though they look the same size, I know one is the baby who makes this call: the two-note whistle of a juvenile red-tail learning to hunt.

Squee-EEE, squee-EEE, squee-EEE! The interval a tritone, unsteady, wild. It is the summer sound I wait for.

The birds bank, circle, trade places in slow motion, rising on widening spirals—two lines that will never converge. Tail feathers glow copper in the sun, and wide wings work without even a flap.

There are no worries while I watch. No questions, no thoughts. Not even a me. Just a pair of hawks in a paradise.

Can't Eat Just One

A surprise island of sunflowers is blooming in the yard. The surprise is that winter squirrels, chipmunks, and white-throated sparrows let so many seeds go uneaten in the grass. I wouldn't have thought this much waste possible, but the evidence is plain. And gorgeous.

I get to watch the show from a lawn chair. The flowers are a living stage for creatures: bees and flies are there to eat pollen and/or nectar; crab spiders and assassin bugs to eat insects who eat pollen and/or nectar; lacewing and ladybug larvae to eat anyone small enough to get eaten; beetles to eat leaves; aphids, spittlebugs to suck sap.

Seeds will be next on the menu. They are forming at the outside rim of the oldest flowers, and seedlets are so new they still wear little beanies of flower parts. But someone has already nibbled the developing fruit—too soon—and the bites reveal innards of whippy fat. Like library paste, if you remember library paste. Or Crisco, if you don't. And if you don't remember Crisco, how about unrefined coconut oil at room temp?

Last week I took a photo at the literal height of bloom, before stalks started to topple. What then looked like heaven now looks like hell. Stems are felling themselves from heads too heavy to hold, and bindweed tugs them minute by minute toward horizontal. On the plus side, some of these flower faces now gaze directly into mine.

I stare at one, hoping to make sense of the math and miracle. It's a green frisbee of Fibonacci spirals with living arcs and whorls, each bump of which will burst into a five-pointed star, but in sequence: outer spirals first, curving toward center. Each star starts male—with pollen—then morphs to female, ready for (someone else's) pollen. If all goes well, star becomes seed.

Which means last winter's leftovers will feed this winter's squirrels, chipmunks, and white-throated sparrows. Right? This is how it is supposed to work.

But my mystery nibbler does not wait for winter. More seedlets are ruined every day. This is not squirrel work. Squirrels drag a flower to the ground, sever the head, carry the head to the fence top; grasp the disc in both hands like a steering wheel; fix me with one eye; and bite, bite, rotate, bite, rotate. More chunks fall out of their mouths than stay in.

One morning at the kitchen window, as I fill the kettle for tea, I see the someone. A female goldfinch. Her breeding plumage is greeny yellow, a camouflage midway between a sunflower's school bus rays and the green bracts beneath them. She selects only withered sunflowers with faces angled down, chins tucked toward stem. She stands on the forehead of a tilted rim and tucks her own head to bite and twist seeds from their pockets. The color match is so close—bird and flower—that if I look away I cannot find her again without a search.

I do search, because I need to watch this beautiful creature "ruin" the seeds I thought I was going to save.

This is how it is supposed to work.

Of the cast of thousands who are busy eating, drinking, and otherwise working our unexpected harvest, she is the star and I am starstruck. I'm her biggest fan.

I still want to watch the warm-up acts. All are limited-time engagements. I want to watch hoverflies hover, and crab spiders crab, and beetles beetle. I want to watch a party of aphids hang from their mouthparts—legs free—and dance synchronized butt shimmies. And it is always a thrill to see spittlebugs fart foam while sucking sap from a leaf axil. But oh, the glory of this green-gold bird. She takes my breath away when she bites that whippy fat, and I find I'm holding a full kettle at the window for so long my arm aches.

"Nothing gold can stay," the poem goes, but maybe she can? Goldfinches haven't nested yet. Most of my neighbors only grow short turf and tidy trees. Maybe she'll see my goldenrod and asters and frostweed and mountain mint—future meals, all—and raise her family here?

Today I see a male goldfinch at it. He is bright gold, a yellow you cannot miss. He is why people call goldfinches "wild canaries." Even on fresh sunflowers there is no camouflage.

He eats from the rims as the female did and does not flinch at the hummingbird who harasses him at speed (too near her feeder), or a Carolina wren. I take photos through our wavy old window to freeze some of the action and beauty, or at least the yellows, greens, and golds.

All because of a few seeds.

From spittlebugs to goldfinches this entire multiact summer spectacular springs from fallen seeds forgotten by winter foragers. It shouldn't astonish me, but it does: how so much—life, death, beauty, occupation—can come from so little.

The happy accident that created this activity was aided, I admit, by lazy lawn care. What if I had mown the seedlings? Or cut flowers when they aged past "pretty"? What if I only grew turf? I'd have fewer eaters, barely a menu, no drama to watch from lawn chair or window, no dinner theater that caters to every taste and every type of mouthpart: to those who sip, sponge, suck, lap, bite, or chew.

The goldfinch "contact call"—the sound they make to one another in flight—is *potato-chip, potato-chip*. Isn't that sweet? But the funny thing is goldfinches make me crave salt, as in super salty *potato-chips, potato-chips*. Lay's Classic Salted comes in bags colored not unlike a male goldfinch in breeding plumage: "wild canary" yellow. Which means year-round, when I see potato chips, they make me crave goldfinches.

Devil's Advocate

Sometimes a place is so important that I can't write about it, because to say a bit is not enough, but to say enough is not possible. "I'll wait until I learn more," or so I think, and I do learn, although the "more" keeps sliding ahead like a bead on a chain. But I need to try. I need to tell you about cedar glades.

"Globally unique" is how the Nature Conservancy describes Middle Tennessee cedar glades. I describe them as ecological mosaics—rare and redneck and beautiful.

Imagine the parking lot of a demolished strip mall: cracked concrete slabs and gravel with a few plants in fissures and edges and wherever snags a scrap of soil. When the sun is low, four colors of shattered glass sparkle as if flung with a broadcast spreader from one barbed wire boundary to the next. Here and there are shotgun shells new, old, and older. Add trash galore, dumped decades ago, ranging in size from roofing nails to a Chevy Nova.

But what if instead of concrete, what you are looking at is bedrock: bare-to-the-sky Ordovician limestone in pavements, sheets, chunks, and clitter, all pitted by erosion and studded with fossils? What if the gravel is native? And what if the stuff growing on and around the gravel is native: lichens, nostoc, mosses, liverworts, sedges, grasses, ferns, cactus, wildflowers? All gorgeous, some rare, and some that only happen here.

"Here" is the bottom of Tennessee's Central Basin. Think of a cereal bowl, and we'd be where the last cornflakes settle after you've slurped from the edge of the Highland Rim. No, think of a colander, because water runs right off the rock into the nearest creek bed or fissure or underground cave or sinkhole large or small. When our state botanist introduces karst topography on hikes, he says, "When you are standing in a cedar glade, you are standing on Swiss cheese."

One time he mentioned that he met the man who owned what is now called Flat Rock Cedar Glades and Barrens, and who can illustrate why glades were used as trash dumps. The man said the woods were good for selling post oak to the broom handle factory. There's chinquapin oak too, which is useful, and blackjack, which at least can burn. But glades? They were a different story. What can you do with bare rock?

"This land ain't good for nothing," the old man told him, "but to keep the sun off the devil's head."

Eventually developers decided rock and gravel weren't so bad. First they came for cropland and pasture. When supplies ran low, they settled for Swiss cheese. Suburban sprawl eats it all, quick. Land is land. Even trash land.

I'd sure love a slice before it's gone for spec homes and gated communities and car dealerships and strip malls. Michael and I dream of our own private cedar glade, our own prairie, our own little oak-hickory woods—the entire glade/barren complex in miniature—but we started dreaming too late and land is priced crazy high.

Is it just as hopeless to dream that smart conservation agencies could buy property adjacent to protected areas? To expand and connect these isolated pockets of "globally unique" land and make sure the remainder isn't smothered in concrete and turf? They'd need a ton of cash and the devil's own luck to jump in ahead of developers.

I wonder what the devil thinks about all of this. I wonder if he misses his old sun hats. And which is more hellish, a cedar glade or a strip mall?

At a Red Light on Music Row

At a red light on Music Row, I saw something weird.

"Hey," I said. "That man. Look. Is he taking a picture of the tree?"

Izzy glanced up from his library book. "Hmm."

"It's a hackberry!" I yelled. "That man *sees* that tree!"

If Music Row is the heart of Nashville's country music business, then the heart of Music Row is the studios along Sixteenth and Seventeenth Avenues. I drive both every school day. Tourists must be surprised that most recording studios are just old houses with old lawns and old trees. I lived in one of those houses back when it was just a house, after college but before I learned to see hackberry trees. Hackberries, I can now argue, are the heart of Nashville, though I don't expect anyone will agree.

One studio is an old church. It is situated at a traffic light that stops us more often than not. Although I remember it as the headquarters for cult televangelist, clothier-to-the-stars, convicted pedophile Tony Alamo, the building is now a big-time studio and a highlight on tours of Music Row. Izzy and I often see the driveway clogged with cargo vans.

But at our red light that morning—a dazzling, hot-green,

early summer morning—the only thing on the driveway was a man. His back was to the sanctuary doors, and he'd raised his arms above his head. He was pointing his phone across Seventeenth toward a humongous hackberry.

This was why I hollered in the car. No one sees hackberry trees. They hide in plain sight: too common, too local, ordinary. Music Row is full of them, but most people only notice the southern magnolias. I used to be one of those people.

The man was about fifty, white, well-fed, in jeans. But why was he taking a photo? Maybe he'd noticed that Music Row had some fine trees? I would so love to make these streets an official arboretum. Maybe it was the mass of English ivy climbing the trunk? Ivy can act as a windsail and take down big trees. Maybe he was documenting this problem? Or maybe he thought ivy was pretty? Most people would.

The tree is one I've watched. It is ordinary and extraordinary, depending. It is just another hackberry, but it surges from the sidewalk to spread itself tall and wide over a squat apartment building. The silhouette is elm-like: a bud vase crammed with arching long-stem flowers plucked from a meadow. There's a smaller hackberry behind it, but from the studio you don't see that second trunk; you just see all the green branches at once, from the same giant vase.

Just then the man turned and threw both arms wide. Someone was coming. It was another man—equally white and well-fed—and the two gave each other a big bro-style, backslapper hug. And then the first man raised his phone high, right where I'd just seen it, at the tree again, and—

quick!—snapped another picture at the moment of this happy reunion.

That's when I realized that the first photo was not aimed at a hackberry tree. That's when I wailed, "Oh, no. It was a selfie! That man didn't see the tree. He was taking a studio selfie. While his friend was coming. And now a double selfie."

As the light turned green, a laugh came from the back seat. "Poor Mom," Izzy said.

I moaned to show Izzy I knew how ridiculous I was. At the red light on Music Row, I was the something weird. But I could not hide my disappointment as I declared to the windshield, as its glittering view offered tree after tree, green heart after heart bursting with summer: "This...had *nothing*...to do...with a hackberry."

Izzy whispered, as he flipped another page, "It never does."

A Dandelion Is to Blow

My Lake City grandmother patrolled her lawn with a quart of Piggly Wiggly bleach: one jug to drench all dandelions. I see her cotton apron and polyester skirt; her mouth a straight line as she dribbles death.

A dandelion is to kill.

My Knoxville grandmother cooked up dandelion greens foraged by her daughter from nearby streets. "Yum," says my aunt, on Facebook, as she shares this memory from seventy years ago.

A dandelion is to eat.

My neighbor—who does not speak English—uproots dandelions from lawns at the sidewalk. She's so good at it that she keeps walking while she bends, yanks, rises, shaking soil from a bouquet of leaves she will take home.

"Is that bad?" worries my son.

A dandelion is to steal.

My boy plucks dandelion clocks: the dry seedballs. Sometimes he squats to break hollow stems low, to minimize movement and keep the fluff firm, but sometimes he grabs as he goes and a trail of down arcs up to his face.

A dandelion is to blow.

≈

Dandelions are on my mind because they are on my lawn. I like them. So did Thoreau, who described early spring dandelions as "the sun itself in the grass."

Recently I reread *A Hole Is to Dig*, by Ruth Krauss and illustrated by Maurice Sendak, to a willing listener. It's a picture book of brief random "first definitions" for children: the essence of what things are as defined by function. "A hole is to dig," "dogs are to kiss people," "ears are to wiggle." Some definitions are quotes from preschoolers. Humming along underneath the dictums, including "a tablespoon is to eat a table with," is a system. I cannot be more specific, but a system there is, and I like it. We should all be so lucky to have a system that supports "mud is to jump in."

Not all kids are captivated with the book's reductive definitions. Mine argued.

"The things they say things are for aren't the only things things are for."

Luckily classroom teachers have set a precedent and have used the book as the starting point it is. Students can riff on the model, generate fresh terms or definitions, and extend the framework.

The entry I'd like to add is dandelion: a dandelion is to blow.

Of course, to blow is not the only thing this thing is for. To define a plant this way is to show my system's hand, whatever it is. It might not be yours. Or that of the dandelion. It wasn't always mine. It certainly wasn't my grandmother's, she of the bleach. That jug is what started me wondering about other functions of dandelions. It led to this: my riff, my oblique extension, relegated to a single artifact.

What is a dandelion?

Dandelion: *n.* a widely distributed weed of the daisy family, with a rosette of leaves, bright yellow flowers followed by globular heads of seeds with downy tufts (*Taraxacum officinale*)—*Concise Oxford English Dictionary*

Not everyone knows that the yellow flower and white ball are the same plant. I've seen adults on hikes point to seed heads and ask "What's that?" And here's a viewer comment from a time-lapse video: "I never knew how these two iterations of the dandelion were related. I thought they were two different flowers! *#blessed*."

A dandelion is to pay attention.

Dandelion anglicizes *dent-de-lion*, tooth of the lion, which describes the leaves, but there are tiny teeth on the achenes as well. Seeds wear barbs that grapple dirt, dog fur, and socks. Which means a seed can fly in air, float on water, plant itself, and walk with four legs or two.

A dandelion is to spread.

The Oxford Dictionary of Phrase and Fable describes dandelion clock as "the downy spherical seed head of a dandelion." Girls blew dandelion clocks to plumb a beloved's heart. If seeds flew, he returned her feelings. If seeds stayed, he did not. No source mentions if boys did this too, when no one was looking.

A dandelion is to pine.

Dandelion seedlings take eight to fifteen weeks to bloom, and after, nine to fifteen days to seed. Pollinators are welcome but not required: "apomictically produced ovules develop into seeds that are genetically identical to the mom plant" (says the blog of my daughter's biology teacher).

A dandelion is to clone.

"Mama had a baby and its head popped off" is what to chant while choking the stem of a dandelion bloom. At "off," flick thumb to decapitate and launch. I did this as a child and forgot until I saw it in an index under "Pastimes; Game Verse; Belief: Plant; Proverbial Comparison." Less creepy games are to hold a flower under the chin of a friend to see if they (a) like butter or (b) are destined for gold.

A dandelion is to play.

Dandelions are weeds, but to insects they are food. Each flower is a hundred smaller flowers that offer pollen and nectar to creatures with little else to eat in our weed 'n' feed lawns, exotic groundcovers, rows of sterile Knock Out roses. It's the first flower of spring, the last of fall, and a surprise in winter.

A dandelion is to bloom.

The United States makes up 40 percent of the world's herbicide market. "Americans have sprayed more than 2.4 billion pounds of glyphosate in the past decade," *Environmental Sciences Europe* reports, but the stats are for Big Agriculture. The rest of us buy Roundup at Home Depot. What are our numbers?

A dandelion is to poison.

Dandelions are old medicine. *Pis en lit* in French and piss-a-bed in English are names that point to roots as diuretic. The botanical name says medicine too: *Taraxacum officinale.* The genus means "disorder," the species "from the pharmacy." For fevers, boils, trouble with eyes, kidneys, livers, warts, low milk supply, and more, depending on where and when you are from.

A dandelion is to cure.

A phone app lets users load an animated dandelion and blow, to puff literal breath onto virtual seed head and watch achenes float out of frame. It costs ninety-nine cents. There are not nearly enough seeds.

A dandelion is to fake.

Dandelion flowers become tea, and by the bucketful, Ray Bradbury's wine. Roasted roots substitute for coffee if absolutely necessary.

A dandelion is to drink.

Tutorials teach how to make paperweights from dandelion seeds: to render heavy that which floats through air. You'll need an empty vending capsule, polyester resin, and a desire to generate nonbiodegradable landfill fodder.

A dandelion is to preserve.

Dandelion seeds do not fly when the weather is wet. Relative humidity must be below 77 percent. Other tricks: leaves exhale a gas to deter nearby species; stems secrete latex to deter pests; taproots can stretch fifteen feet, and, if broken, can grow a new plant from each fragment.

A dandelion is to succeed.

Rubber plantations replace rainforests, but dandelion

latex can replace rubber, and without robbing the world of a single bird or butterfly. Test: coat finger with dandelion latex, let dry, roll it down the fingertip, and voilà—a rubber band.

A dandelion is to stretch.

Dandelions came to North America on purpose: a sure thing for medicine and food. The vitamin C could cure scurvy on the journey.

A dandelion is to immigrate.

Hummingbirds weave seed fluff into nests. Not on the outside, where white silk can advertise, but on the inside, where the female shapes the down with her breast. Both of my children have felt ruby-throated heartbeats against their palms. Do they remember?

A dandelion is to cradle.

Dandelion imagery blooms in self-help language and developmental psychology. "Dandelion children" are resilient, but "orchid children" are vulnerable.

A dandelion is to metaphor.

When my older kid was little I stopped her from blowing dandelions near driveway cracks, the vegetable patch, the herb garden. Next time she visits from college, I will invite her to make up for lost fluff.

A dandelion is to redeem.

Dandelion flowers dragged by a child against pavement make yellow marks. When hammered onto cotton, a dye. Boiled roots make orange, and the whole plant makes maroon. In Minecraft, dandelion dye is a renewable resource in survival mode.

A dandelion is to color.

Kids still wish on dandelions. Some sources say it must be the first dandelion of spring. Some say a wish comes true only if "whiskers are gone after the third puff." Some don't say anything because the only rule is no rules.

A dandelion is to wish.

I wish I had found a dandelion for my mother-in-law on her final visit. At eighty-five, she was a dandelion virgin, and so she remains.

She sat in our cheap lawn chair like a queen, and we filled her cupped hands with pretty things out of reach. No dandelions had gone to seed at the moment, and when I described them and what they were for, she didn't understand.

"I'm a city girl," she said. "This is not my culture."

Even city girls should know what it is to snap a dandelion stalk,

print a circle on a fingertip with the hollow straw,

lift fluff to lips,

heave one spitting blast,

watch parachutes fly, float, fall.

Dandelions tell time. The yellow opens with sunrise and closes with dusk, but the seedball is the famous "clock." We are to count how many puffs it takes to bald it, to rip every seed loose from its moorings.

One o'clock, two o'clock, three...

I wish we had more time.

Because a dandelion is to blow.

It Was a Yellow-Billed Cuckoo

My mom recently moved to a senior community a long drive from my house but a short drive to my favorite cedar glade. Last night she let me sleep on the sofa so I could start a hike before dawn, and I've snuck to my car under a black and quiet sky.

A Dodge pickup tails me on new asphalt past new subdivisions (so many) and old pasture (not so many), but when he turns toward the interstate I turn away. Pink begins to glow through my open window.

Now I'm passing fields of hay bales, the big round kind, and I smell them on swirls of surprisingly cool air. It's late July and each is surrounded by a sea of grass already tall. Is hay cut-and-come-again or once-is-done? I don't know anyone to ask.

The sign at the parking lot says "open 7 a.m.," which means I'm illegal, but I cannot miss this chance of sunrise and solitude. Eastern towhees sing from persimmon trees for me to *Drink my tea, tea, tea*. Five syllables. Like the mourning dove from a red cedar farther on, but a dove is slow and sad: *Coo-wee-hooo, hoo, hoo*. No wonder people hear "owl" in predawn dove.

At the fork I walk to the right so Tennessee coneflowers will face me. The pink rays are faded, tired. It wasn't an on year for them, like it was the summer after the drought, right after they were taken off the federal endangered list. It's thanks to the coneflower that the Nature Conservancy bought this land and transferred it to the state. Saving one charismatic species means saving the rare ecosystem that supports it: cedar glade and xeric limestone prairie.

And then I hear something new. A repeated call like a hoot, but not the dove and not any owl I know. It's more like a car alarm than a bird. Hollow and reedy and shockingly loud. The sequence is one pitch barked at an even tempo, unrushed, about six times, then a lower note for a few more: *Ka-ka-ka-ka-ka-ka-kow-kow-kowlp!*

I must see this. But as I jog through a glade to get closer, I realize it's coming from far past the cedar thickets. Beyond the tall limestone beds and barbed wire. The only animals I've heard make this tone and volume are white-cheeked gibbons at the Nashville zoo. What Davidson County creature could possibly sound like a rainforest primate?

Sun pops over the cedars behind me. My sudden shadow stretches over the rocks—the trail is a creek bed when called for—and I'm as tall as the winged elm I walk toward but comically thin. I breathe cedar perfume, dirt, sumac, the tea spice of glade calamint.

No wetness in the wet-weather wash, just cracked sheets of soil with scrolled edges. But even dry, the limestone pavement bleeds gorgeous gradations of color: buffs and greens and rubbings of iron red.

Warm enough for cicadas before seven a.m. They buzz in waves with wide vibrato, slow, then fast, then faster, then silence. Then again.

What I call Shotgun glade has the best view of glass shards in low sun: clear, green, amber, brown, and the prize of cobalt blue. Wedged under pads of pricky pear cactus are old friends—the Avon bottle, the Comet can lid; rusted tips of 12-gauge shells; a handful of fat nails the color of ripe honey locust pods. Antique trash tells a story of how this land was used. There's a GM chassis in the little bluestem by the river oats and the drum of a 1950s washing machine off-trail near the mullein, near where glade cress blooms in rock basins for weeks.

At Hawk glade I sit in shade, in gravel, in lance leaf gumweed. Michael and I named this glade for the time we realized our toddler was no longer behind us, and we backtracked and found him on a rock, staring at the sky. "Hawk," he explained.

A lone star tick tickles the back of my neck. This is one I won't have to pull later.

I'm getting hungry. And sunburned. The migraine starts. It is as expected as the trash, the ticks, the gumweed.

There is commuter traffic on the way back to Mom's, where I de-tick and shower and find clean clothes. She has timed a breakfast of home fries with scrambled eggs hot and buttery and has filled a Ziploc with ice for my head. I will spend the afternoon trying to figure out who yelled in the woods like a white-cheeked gibbon, but now, with Mom's blessing, I take my plate to her porch so I can eat alone underneath a corner of the bluest sky.

What a Butterfly Means

At book group someone asked *why write about nature*, and someone answered *we write to make meaning*.

But what if meaning is already there?

Let's say I see a butterfly in the rain at Warner Park and it's a Gulf fritillary that has only been a butterfly for a moment. It hangs from its empty casing to let gravity stretch what had been sausage-packed. I see bronze and white and a smidge of gold but no orange. Orange stays secret until wings fly.

Let's say the butterfly is trellised from rain above and below by tutored stems of its own host plant: Tennessee's native passion vine, *Passiflora incarnata*. Weeks ago, when the butterfly hatched as a 2 mm caterpillar (and ate its own eggshell), it pigged out on this plant. It survived every predator as it ate leaf after larger leaf; as it sloughed four tight skins (and ate those too); as its turds grew from invisible to the size of kosher salt; as it chose a likely spot to spin enough silk to anchor its butt to the top of the trellis, and to dangle as a letter J to whiten and twinkle and boil and heave and then unzip one last caterpillar outfit up, up, and off until the old skin fell—a bristly mask—to the dirt below.

As chrysalis, it fooled chipmunk, wasp, skink, bird.

Let's say this all happened because if it hadn't, the butterfly wouldn't be here.

I'm here.

I'm here at the passion vine in the nature center's organic garden, with my husband and our boy, who are hollering at me to "Come try a pepper" and who answer my "What kind" with "The sign says ornamental."

Let's say I leave the butterfly some privacy while it figures out its new body parts and new purpose, that I wish it well, and that I pull the wet wooden gate to find out if ornamental peppers are more than just, you know, ornamental.

Fameflower

Finally, a fameflower. *Phemeranthus calcaricus.*

For years I've found the fleshy foliage, the seedpods, and the buds, but never the flower. You'd think hot pink would scream *Here I am!*, in a limestone glade. Fameflower is Dollar Store sippy-cup pink, Barbie pink, the same pink my daughter refused to wear after age four. But somehow fameflower whispers.

Maybe because the flower face is smaller than a dime and waves atop a three-inch invisible stem. Maybe because to bloom it needs full afternoon sun, and when afternoon sun is full in a cedar glade I am half-blind with bright sky mirrored by pale rock, and with sun blinking from decades of broken bottles.

But nothing else could have gotten me down on my belly to count petals and memorize yellow stamens. Direct from the gravel is the only height to take a decent photo of fameflower from, which I tried though the screen glared black and my glasses slid off from sweat, and though I knew there'd be ticks to pull later. Also splinters from prickly pear. It was worth it. Not because the photos were decent—they were as overexposed as I was—but because they were proof of victory.

And they caught what the flowers sprang from. Native gravel mostly, with crisps of nostoc and the black lichen everyone thinks is tar at first, but there was trash too. Fameflower bloomed between thick chunks of old glass and thin shards of beer bottles, from pull tabs and light bulb bases and rusted shotgun shells. Over toward any edge with a whisper of deeper soil they grew near glade moss, pincushion moss, hairy lip fern. The milieu of fameflower.

I was warned the fameflower "window" was three to five p.m. Before and after, they'd be shut. This is the same window I'd prefer to spend inside an air-conditioned house. Nashville was ninety-eight today, which would put cedar glades several degrees higher. Sun locks itself inside rocks too hot to rest a hand on.

Michael and Izzy came with me. Neither cared about fameflowers beyond polite support of my quest, but they figured recent rains would make a good show at the sinkhole. They left me and headed toward water.

But then, "Fameflowers, Jo!" The yell came from behind a wall of cedars.

I started to run, but Michael's voice came from the grass: a pocket of prairie, not a glade.

"Is yours a hot pink or a pale pink?" I yelled at the cedars.
"Pale!"

"Is it growing in a tall readymade bouquet?"
"Yes."

"It isn't fameflower and I can't remember the name right now, but y'all go on and I'll meet you at the sinkhole."

Michael's flower in the prairie pocket was rose pink,

also called rose gentian (*Sabatia angularis*). I remembered the name after we'd sweated and gasped our way back to the car. Rose pink is an absolute glory of its own, but those blooms stay open for days. Fameflower chooses its moment, and I needed to be in that moment.

Fameflowers were likelier in the glass—not grass—like what crunched under my feet beside the prickly pear right after Michael yelled. I was exactly where glade cress grows in early spring: drifts of pink and yellow and white, smelling of honey and busy with butterflies. So I slowed down, looked down. And that's when I saw it, my first fameflower.

The genus name means "ephemeral," because the blooms only last a day. I don't know who came up with "fame." It's been famously elusive to me. Native plant nerds know it is designated state-endangered, and the habitat is disappearing fast. But at Couchville Cedar Glade, which is small but protected and managed, it is "locally abundant." It's here that Jason the park ranger—the one who gave me the heads-up about the window—said he'd counted 175 fameflower blooms in one day. I nearly died of jealousy, having found zero the day before. But isn't it great that someone counts fameflower blooms? Not for a survey but for fun?

My first fameflower was by a landmark wheel of prickly pear. This is the monster clump of native cactus near the stream, and in May it fires up flowers easy to see: big, wide yellow petals with red throats and a mess of yellow stamens and so many bees.

I squat here at Couchville year-round, flowers or no. It's in an expanse of pavement best enjoyed in low sun so rays can scatter themselves across more glass than you knew was there. And best in midday sun so pitiless that you have to spend the next two days in a dark bedroom with ice Velcro-ed to your head. Also best with dawn birdsong different from what you hear at home. And best in the evening when you have to shush your family long enough to giggle at how narrow-mouthed toads bleat like lambs. It is always best.

For future reference, it's the cactus clump with the Comet lid. The lid could well be Ajax or Bon Ami, but I know for sure it's a metal disc that in a former life topped a cardboard canister of scouring powder. The stamped words that curve with the rim say, "For Sinks & Pots & Pans & Tubs." I wouldn't be surprised if the Pots & Pans it scoured are here now, buried in one of the berms of rusted metal. Or the Sink & Tub, for that matter.

I check that Comet lid at least once a season, to see what might be growing through the holes. One time it was glade cress. Maybe next year a fameflower? I keep pushing it under the cactus pads so no one else will see it. I'm afraid they'll think it is trash.

Why It Is Good to Go Outside
Even If You Feel Like Hell

It is good to go outside even if you feel like hell.

Outside is about the hummingbird butting his head into the shut morning glories for one last lick. It's about the butterfly who stops fluttering long enough to swing upside down on the pipe vine—her one and only host plant—to squeeze out seven eggs in neat rows, one orange speck at a time.

Outside is not about you. Or your pain. But even though you are no use to anyone or yourself and the day is too hot, bright, loud, and crooked, you are outside. Good.

Outside are things to hear:

chickadee (*feebee feebay*)

Carolina wren (*teakettle teakettle*)

cicada chorus in 2/4 time

cars passing the porch

interstate roar

the neighbor's TV (*Star Trek*)

cicada distress call (*don't eat me, don't eat me*)

cardinal (*birdy, birdy*)

Nature is not here just to teach you or cure you or remind you of something about yourself, though you can, of course, learn and heal and remember—which we all desperately need to do—but that's not why this bee is biting a circle from the redbud leaf, or why the pokeweed is blooming, or why a cottontail is stretching and rolling in the dirt by the porch where rain never reaches.

Outside are things to see:

monarch on the pink zinnia

carpenter bee on the passionflower

skippers, too quick to ID

cherry tomatoes round and red

yellowed hackberry leaves falling

dew for some reason still twinkling in the grass

wind moving just the top of the sugar maple

two and now three hummingbirds fighting, squeaking
     in mid-air

and this big black wasp on the bare dirt at your feet, scraping at it a full three minutes before taking off slowly, weighted, resolute, straight up, up, up until your neck won't let your face follow her into the noonday sun.

Ticked Off

Izzy's new soccer field became a park only last year. To get there we had to drive on I-65 to the ever-expanding mall town of Cool Springs, then exit to a parallel road in the opposite direction. We passed fresh warehouses, a building supply company, and an Audi dealership that takes up gosh knows how many acres of prior pasture and found Flagpole Park gasping in the sun. Landscaping had been in the budget, but I don't think watering was.

Looking northeast from the parking lot, I can see the famous 1930s WSM radio tower, home of the Grand Ole Opry. I love that tower. I love the symmetry and the denial of gravity. All those cables holding a giant skinny diamond at rest on its point. It reeks of optimism. The soccer game did not.

Izzy attached himself to friends, so I walked a few yards from the sideline up a short grassy bank, past some recently planted and already dying redbuds, to the chain-link fence. And there was the interstate below. I could easily drop a ball—or anything—onto the southbound lanes. The fence was lined with what grows where no one trims: bush honeysuckle, red cedars, Bradford pear, hackberry, black cherry. Orange dirt shone beneath the cedars, as did full dog bags and empty drink cans.

A bleach jug told me the oldest trash is probably all that remains of the white farmhouse that used to sit where the soccer field is now. I bet someone at that farm watched the radio tower rise taller and taller, bracket by bracket. Decades later, what did the dynamite feel like when I-65 split soybean fields into two cliffs and a canyon? And again later, when four lanes weren't enough?

Next to the trees struggled wild prairie tea, and I rubbed the leaves to smell my fingers. Queen Anne's lace was about to go to seed, but hedge parsley already had. It held bristled burrs in candelabras of seed. When I looked down, dozens of burrs had spiked themselves to my jeans.

It is all sun at this park, unless you thought to bring an umbrella with the folding soccer chair you also remembered, so five or six of us slacker parents sat flat on the grass in the one scrap of shade the fence line offered.

But sitting on the ground in my black jeans exposed my white ankles. And on these ankles were tick bites from two days before. And on these, for the entire soccer game, were flies. Two flies decided my ankles were the most fascinating things at Flagpole Park. For forty-five minutes they flew to and from my swollen spotted skin, and every time they landed, they tickled. And every time they tickled, they triggered a bigger itch.

What you need to understand is that there were fifty-seven tick bites on the left leg and twenty-nine on the right. This breaks a new personal best/worst, and I hadn't even counted the bites on my arms and back and other body parts. What kills me is that most of the bites were nibbles; the ticks didn't have time to attach. A pinprick of tick slobber is enough to inflame my skin into fat angry welts.

Let me back up. At Owl's Hill Nature Sanctuary two days prior, I took a lovely hike with Gail and Richard, my naturalist buddies. Before I got in my car to drive home, I whipped out my adhesive lint roller—as usual—to check for ticks. The first swipe down my leg picked up dozens of the tiniest possible tick babies, freshly hatched.

And here's where a lovely hike morphs into horror.

I rolled through four changes of adhesive, and each caught about fifty hatchlings. When I peeped in my socks there were more, plus bigger nymphs already engaged, so I smooshed the lint roller all over my ankles, between my toes. I threw shoes and socks into a plastic bag, tied a knot, then drove barefoot straight home to detox with a Silkwood shower. After which ticks were roaming the bottom of the tub.

Even then Michael had to duct tape more free-range ticks off my arms, back, belly, side, legs, butt. Because, you see, hatchlings are too tiny to scrape with a fingernail. This is what happens when you walk through a swarm of tick babies if you don't wear enough repellent and if you are a tick magnet.

I am a tick magnet. Not only for horror movie larvae fests

but for your average everyday deer tick and lone star tick. As a kid at camp, I'd get three a day. It is rare to lint roll myself after any hike and not pick up several. I've gotten ticks every month of the year except January. I've gotten ticks in my own yard, and I live in town. I regularly support three stages of tick life—larva, nymph, and adult—and they all adore me. Mosquitos and chiggers too. Not only do I get more bites than anyone else with me at the time, my body overreacts to the toxins.

I'll be wearing these spots for months.

This is why I do not understand when adults admit that they have never had a tick. Five grownups who feature in my life have said this, and they are people who have been outside, owned pets, and lived through at least three full decades on this planet.

"How do ticks work?" one friend asked. "Do they just bite and leave, or do they stay?"

I could barely trust myself to respond. I felt shock, wonder, and then rage. It still ticks me off. What must it be like to be that innocent? How is it possible? Even without firsthand experience, how can an educated person be that shielded from popular culture, news reports, magazine articles, flea collar ads, any random source that might have mentioned how ticks work?

My dark side, the side fueled by a half century of tick saliva, wants to answer my friend's question by dropping her into the middle of a waist-high midsummer meadow.

≈

So by the time of the soccer game, my bites had had time to redden and swell. The ankles were the worst; and sun, heat, grass, and flies exacerbated every welt. The urge to scratch grew. The urge to claw, scrape, abrade, excoriate gradually eclipsed the game and all societal norms. I could no longer resist. And here is where those hedge parsley burrs came in handy.

When I lost control, fingertips were not enough. Fingernails were not enough. They teased. So I plucked the dried burrs off my jeans, held them flat in my hand, and rubbed them into my ankles. Hard.

And why stop there? Why not pick up a nearby palm-sized chunk of limestone not studded with tiny fossils but made entirely of fossils: ridged, broken shards of little Ordovician sea creatures. The chunk had slept underground until a year ago, when a not deep enough hole was shoveled to plant a redbud tree. But now the rock was mine, and congealed, lithified bodies would scrape my own. If I'd had two rocks, I'd have buffed my calf bone like a shoeshine.

Flies had little chance to land now, what with a stone sliding round and round each anklebone, smearing pus and blood along puffed contours between jeans and sandal. Reckless ecstasy, that's what it was. The limestone was salvation, even though I knew there'd be histamine hell to pay.

No one noticed. All eyes were turned toward our boys, who were so overpowered by an older team that they hardly advanced out of their half of the field. At the last whistle I jumped up and stuffed the rock in my purse, my ankles on fire.

It was a good thing I took that chunk of limestone. What I didn't notice—not that anyone can until it is too late—was that the grass we were sitting on was prime chigger habitat.

And if you don't know how chiggers work, I will save a seat just for you, flat on the ground at Flagpole Park.

Ghost Rain

Each individual plant-louse may produce
from five to seven drops of honeydew in
twenty-four hours. If our cows could produce
as much in proportion, then a good Holstein
would give something like six thousand
pounds of milk per day.

ANNA BOTSFORD COMSTOCK,
Cornell Nature Study Leaflet XXI

What would you call a thing you see for the first time, a thing you knew happened all summer, a thing you've seen the results of for years but never actually watched because you thought it was invisible? What would you call that? A miracle? Or at least a big deal?

Honeydew is falling from the hackberry tree. Slower than rain. Smaller and less determined. It behaves more like the tiniest of snowflakes. Or a mist, super fine. Some droplets fall straight, some angle south with the barely there breeze. In counterpoint to both, white woolly aphids float from where the mist comes. Aphids waft in dozy trajectories: up, down, sideways. Little aphids look big when you are trying to see honeydew.

Do you know honeydew? Not the green melon but the stuff aphids make while they suck your garden dry. Honeydew is aphid poo.

The crown of this native hackberry spans twenty feet of driveway. Honeydew is falling from under every leaf as usual, but the honeydew I can see falls from one section of crown, where the action is lit in contrast to the dark asphalt of Next Door's roof. The sun's top edge is directly over her ridge vent, and for a few moments it blazes through a screening of hackberry leaves and then through me. So the players are sun, tree, roof, and insect; and though the show isn't new, I'm watching it for the first time.

I saw it at all because of a bird. A shudder on the ridgeline turned out to be a young cardinal in front of the sun. After I'd worked this out, a new field of movement slid into view: a layer, a sheet, a perpendicular transparency like a backdrop loosed from the catwalk onto a stage. It invited me. I needed to be inside it. At first I walked toward the sheet and blinded myself. Then I stood blinking in the direct path of sun and honeydew, arms out, palms up, to catch the drops. But I couldn't feel anything: me, who feels things no one around me can, like seed ticks inching up my wrist or dust mite bites in bed. I fetched a glass plate from the kitchen, ran back, held the plate level under the tree, and there they were: the tiniest of droplets. Little pinprick dots on the glass. I licked them. Sweet. Honeydew. Sugar from aphid butts is raining on me, and I can see it *and* taste it.

These are Asian woolly hackberry aphids, but all aphids produce honeydew because they all suck plants. They take nutrients and excrete the extras. And guess where the extras exit? The anus. Which means honeydew really is aphid excreta or waste or, if you will, poo. What is trash to aphids is treasure to insects appreciative of sweet. You've probably heard how ants can "farm" aphids, how ants can supply security services in exchange for meals of on-demand honeydew. If an aphid predator comes around—say, an aphid lion or the larva of a syrphid fly—ants protect the herd. And when an ant wants feeding, she has only to stroke an aphid to stimulate what in human biology we would call peristalsis. *Plop.*

Too many people here in Nashville hate hackberry trees (long story for another time), but most haters don't make the direct connection with honeydew. Haters know to connect the tree to summer's black goo that cloaks all nearby things: the roof, the siding, the driveway, and so on. The black stuff isn't honeydew; it's the sooty mold that grows on the honeydew. The more honeydew, the more black mold. The more black mold, the more hackberry hate. I'm glad few people connect the goo to bugs, because when they do they reach for systemic pesticides or foliar applications, and then all insects die, including predators who eat aphids. Agricultural extension bulletins admit you can't control (i.e., kill) Asian woolly aphids, so why try? They are a consequence you must accept when you choose a house with a hackberry near it, and in Nashville this means nearly every house.

These bugs were accidentally brought from China, where they specialize in Chinese hackberries and do no harm. Now they specialize in ours. Turn over the nearest hackberry leaf and it will likely be populated with woollies. They wear shreds of white wax that fluff onto your fingertip if you decide to investigate. They will not defecate on command no matter how convincingly you pretend to be an ant.

I am not immune to sooty mold hate. I hate that it coats the hackberry and the five pawpaws I stupidly planted underneath. It coated the plastic turtle sandbox every year until no amount of bleach and bristle could clean it. It coats the driveway, flowerpots, gutters, and the car. When ink coats the enormous passion vine I wonder if the butterfly larvae who depend on passion vine as their sole food source dread the moment when vines show more black than green. Do the caterpillars grimace while they chew? Do they wish I'd take a nailbrush and scrub? After a string of dry days if you bend a vine, the black cracks and you can peel it from the green in strips.

Still, I wouldn't dream of killing all of my insects with poison to destroy the one species that invites the mold. I don't even want all of the woolly aphids dead. Everything—our entire food web—depends on insects. Other invertebrates need to eat, as do birds and reptiles and amphibians and mammals. As do we.

Sugar is forbidden on my new migraine diet. No starches, no fruit. The sweetest thing allowed is blueberries a couple of times a week. I am dying to know the carb count of aphid honeydew. Judging by exploratory licks, it is as sweet as maple syrup, molasses, brown rice syrup, as sweet as honey.

And look at all the time and labor it takes to produce those sweet things. Look how hard bees have to work to make honey. Aphids make theirs by taking a dump.

In *A Natural History of North American Trees*, Donald Culross Peattie calls aphid honeydew "ghost rain," and you can see why: because you can't see it. Not usually. Not unless you accidentally discover the perfect angle of sun-through-tree from a lawn chair in the driveway.

Seeing the unseen is one answer I could offer to Mary Oliver's question in her poem "The Summer Day." It is what I "plan to do" with my "one wild and precious life." I will look for big deals. I will look for other wild lives around me, and I will learn where I am. Like when I see Gulf fritillary caterpillars on their passion vine hatch,

eat,

molt,

bleed,

excrete,

puke,

pupate,

eclose,

fly,

mate,

lay eggs,

die.

These are words in one sentence, but it took years to see them all, and each stage was big.

Hearing bats in our backyard was a big deal, especially when for twenty years we didn't know we had bats.

Watching a bumblebee fall asleep at dusk and wake at dawn under the same milkweed leaf six days in a row? Big deal.

Watching a spotted orb weaver spin her enormous web, eat her enormous web.

Watching a leaf-cutting bee scribe a wee circle from a redbud leaf.

Watching pink strings on a dead possum's belly sort themselves into tails attached to hidden, hungry orphans.

And here's another big deal, though I hesitate to mention it because when viewed alongside my aphid excretions it may suggest an obsession with the scatological, but the truth is nature is messy.

It was a June morning years ago, in a sunny meadow at Cedars of Lebanon State Park, when my family happened upon a patch of exposed limestone. We stopped, we stared.

"A dung beetle," our five-year-old said, "rolling a ball of poo." And then louder but still deadpan, he announced, "This is the greatest day of my life."

I remember yelling, "Dung beetles? In Wilson County? I thought they were in Africa!" I remember posting the three-second video and getting no likes, no comments, and thinking, "Oh my Lord, I must be so strange," but also, "This is an out-and-out miracle and I wish I could share it better."

I wished everyone in the world could stand in the sunny, tick-y glade to watch beetles shape coyote scat into a ball and roll it uphill and backward and could marvel that the female will lay eggs in that ball so hatchlings will have a good first meal. I wished we could all freak out that dung beetles way down here by our feet orient themselves by the stars. By the stars! If we had to orient by the stars we'd be lost, literally, but these bugs who roll shit can do it, are born to do it, are born in a ball of dung to do it.

What joy to witness secrets weird and wonderful. What a big deal to see creatures doing their thing, busy with their own wild and precious lives, oblivious to mine.

Some friends of ours want to move from Nashville to Wyoming, to live under a big sky. I checked a range map, and hackberries do not grow in Wyoming. Our friends vacation there, and "life is short," and they want to "wake up every day to mountains and valleys," which would be a big deal, no question. They'd be able to ski right out the door. I understand. But I like living under a small sky. I like waking up every day to our city yard, our hackberries. I like to sit with my teacup right here in a blackened folding chair on our blackened driveway. And to watch honeydew shoot from a million aphid assholes.

Fall

Soccer Ecotone

Zones of overlap, or ecotones, between two
habitats are often richer in species than either
habitat.

JENNY OWEN,
New Scientist

Soccer mom here at five p.m. practice, late August, hoping
the breeze holds. I am crisscross-applesauce on the bench
farthest from the sun and the shouting. Fourth-grade boys
talk in shrieks.

Male cicadas buzz. They sing in ratcheting crescendos
from trees that carve schoolyard from city: catalpas, hackberries, elms. Underneath is the ubiquitous accidental
hedge of exotic honeysuckle and privet. The funny thing is
that even the native trees are accidental, stretching straight
out the top of a wide stone wall. The limestone is snugged
by chain-link on the school side, but the city side is a six-
foot drop to a service alley for a mixed-use high-rise.

Bare bellies in assorted colors and curves patrol the field.
One will forget his T-shirt in the grass.

Dragonflies patrol. They must have hatched in the outdoor classroom by the fence, in the artificial pond. Where

would the next nearest habitat be? A storm sewer? A fountain at Vanderbilt University? The famous guitar-shaped swimming pool on Music Row? The insects are too far from my bench to ID, and I'm too tired to unpretzel my legs and walk closer. Too tired to confirm the poison ivy I'm warned is sieving itself through chain-link mesh. But shouldn't kids—even city kids—already know what poison ivy looks like?

They know vine honeysuckle and how to suck the honey. It'll bloom on the fence toward the end of the school year— not the beginning, not now. Who tells them to pinch the green knob just so, and to pull the string slow, to rake nectar through the hole, to lick the clear bead?

Movement pulls my eye toward the playground, up past the towers of the wooden fort, way up in the cooling breeze. Elm leaves—always the first to go—tumble and dart. Dozens sail over the parking lot, and for half a second, half a breath, I can't tell dragonfly from leaf, can't tell summer from fall.

Cotton Candy Is a Constant

Leftover cotton candy doesn't keep, even in a twist-tied bag. Humidity invades, fibers compress, but a little density doesn't deflate all the magic. A dense cloud is still a cloud, and what's not to love about biting a cloud?

Another magic thing about cotton candy is how happy it makes our son to have it, and to eat too much at once. I don't even mind when he spits on it ("a science experiment") to collapse a hank of air into rock, as long as he doesn't spit directly into the bag, which he would if he could.

I open yesterday's bag from the Tennessee State Fair. The pink is gone, but astride the blue is one tiny dermestid beetle, the varied carpet beetle you've seen at home if you've got good eyes. They are one-sixteenth of an inch long. I'm guessing she's female because females wander in search of a tasty spot in which to lay eggs (hatchlings are notorious pantry pests). What is the more likely backstory, that she toppled into the machine and got spun inside a pastel cocoon the size of a human head, through which she has finally eaten an exit, or that last night she tunneled from my Formica countertop through a gap in the twist-tie? I tap her onto the front lawn and do not stay to watch her land because cotton candy is calling.

I'm pretty sure each of the past twenty-six state fairs has been smaller than the one before. It compresses. Michael and I both remember, but we remind each other when the midway spilled through the tunnel and way on down the hill, when 4-H tobacco and hay and soybeans took up twice the floor space, when the rabbit barn didn't need to double up with poultry, and when Hoot Owl Junction had a string band and a steam-powered gristmill and the molasses mule and the loom lady. We remember when the entomology exhibit included specimens in glass vials and a glue trap of brown recluses, and how nobody stole them. Or maybe somebody did steal them and that's why they stopped showing up.

Some things at the fair are better. More skin colors. More headscarves for religion, not just for pretty. No beer means fewer fights after sundown. I haven't seen anyone wearing a Confederate flag since 2008.

It's true that you have to hunt for vendors who spin cotton candy onboard the trailer, who don't simply hang full sacks from the eaves. Hardly any are set up to offer the original and preferred presentation of handing you a fresh flyaway wad on a stick.

But still, cotton candy is a constant.

When my sisters and I were little, Mom brought wet washcloths in baggies to our Knoxville fair specifically for cotton candy cleanup. This was before baby wipes, before Ziplocs. Sometimes we supplemented by tipping paper cones of free Baptist water over our hands, but out of sight of the Baptists, in case it was rude to wash with water meant for mouths.

I learned last year to avoid the yellow. Some misguided marketer at some cotton candy headquarters decided yellow should be lemon flavored. Lemon? Lemon belongs in -ade, in drops, in curd, as slices on a lox platter. My family are purists for pink and blue. But if yellow is lemon, what flavor is pink? What flavor is blue? Do you know? I didn't, and I never even wondered until now.

Pink and blue turn out to be vanilla and raspberry respectively. And I have now learned that cotton candy was invented here in Nashville, in 1897, which is delightful, and by a dentist, which is funny.

Yesterday, as we drove out of the fairgrounds lot, waved across the grass by workers in safety vests, an ancient man stopped us. He was Black. We are white. We will wonder later what this man's fair was like twenty-six years ago, and twenty-six years before that, and twenty-six before that.

He looked down at our blue-mouthed, blue-fingered boy in the booster seat and said, "You going to have a stomachache tonight with all that cotton candy." I think he was about to joke that we should give him some—the man, I mean—but by then I'd already raised the bag up through the window and, surprising all of us, offered loud: "The pink's better than the blue. Have some pink." And he did.

Leaf Prints

I am squatting on the sidewalk in front of a duplex down the street when a guy in white painter's pants walks out the door and sees me. In his hand is a paint roller.

"What's up?" he asks, in a not unfriendly yell.

"Leaf prints!" I yell back, which he doesn't understand, and why should he? Beef prince! Deep rinse! Geek blintz! Any similar-sounding words could be as likely.

On the sidewalk are prints of leaves, but no leaves. Yesterday's rain "painted" them, and the morning's breeze blew away the originals. Nature's monoprints are under my feet.

Here is red maple. It is a fat brown trident. Here is one with a missing point. Here are pin oak silhouettes from the condo across the street. Here are deep curves that say a bur oak grows nearby. All are in sepia tones, with dark edges where the dye stayed longest. Here are crape myrtle capsules too heavy to fly so they sit on their own sooty shadows. And here are only echoes of leaves—elm, maybe—that shifted while they bled.

The best prints are on clean concrete still porous and

pale enough to suck pigment. Add a dead leaf. Add rain. Leaf tannins transfer themselves to the sidewalk, then get baked by sun. This makes found art. Nature's paint.

Tannin is what's also in tea, wine, acorns, bark. It tans animal skin, bites it from rawhide to tough leather. And it stains sidewalks with signs of fall.

When the man walks near enough to see what I'm pointing to, he laughs and says, "Oh, those. Yeah. It won't take more than a minute with a pressure washer."

"No, I like them—"

"I've got one on the truck—"

We speak at the same time while looking at the same thing, though we do not see it the same way. I want to capture the art. He wants to wash it away.

"They're pretty," I finish.

"But I'm just here to paint," he says, walking back to his job, his shrug a full stop.

Field Trip Leavings

One of the things I love about Warner Park's Meadow Tree trail is how it can accommodate a walker who is both inquisitive and lazy. I am proof. The trail starts near the nature center and meanders between woods and driveway, flanked by trees young enough to offer low branches for inspection. Buds and leaf scars are usually within reach. Most trees wear name tags. In between, requiring no extra effort, no additional travel, I am kept company by wildflowers galore, including passion vine, milkweed, snakeroot, wingstem, and goldenrod, all in the fruiting stage and a banquet for seedeaters.

Today's goal was to fondle fallen leaves of the fifty-one specimens on the trail. Well, my bigger goal is still to know trees—every part of every tree—how they look, smell, and taste (when appropriate); how people and animals use them; how they function; where they're from; where they grow best. Everything about a tree.

Examining fallen leaves is one path to knowing. I see how colors change, I feel textures above and below—roughleaf dogwood is aptly named—I notice stems, how a leaf behaves once it's down.

Sycamore leaves are dinner plates in the grass, with stem ends so big and hollow they could be goblets for Barbies.

Sweetgum stars point from leaf litter in reds, yellows, browns, eggplant purple. They look like paint chip samples at a store.

Hackberry leaves curl into nothings.

Winged sumac leaflets are impossibly red: absolute shockers.

On the way to the trail I squatted by the wonder twins, the two backcross-bred legacy chestnut babies engineered to be as American as apple pie but as blight resistant as Chinese chestnuts. I can only imagine the decades of work that resulted in these trees, and how chestnut-mad devotees figured out a sustainable way to resurrect a giant. I fingered the leaves puddled beneath their rebar cage with respect, even reverence. I was already on my knees, after all.

I also felt weird, as if I were hiding from the school field trips nearby. I had a clear view of Warner naturalists doing their miraculous thing, the most important thing: introducing children to nature, helping them see signs of the season. And where was I? Hunkered alone behind a screen of baby trees, petting leaves.

The trees let leaves go, but I want to keep them. All of them. I don't have room, and besides, no one can collect anything in a Metro Park. My instinct is to stuff them into grocery bags, organize them, use them somehow, honor them. And to remember where each came from, and when—the when being right now.

To remember when sun stretched the cancer scar along my cheekbone.

To remember when a zillion multicolored ladybugs bumbled into my bag, pockets, hair, mouth.

To remember the smell of squashed persimmons on the new sidewalk.

And the silvered shadows on honey locust thorns.

And the garter snake stare down near the tulip poplar.

To remember the rare treat of a solo field trip to anywhere, but especially to here, one of my favorite places in the world.

Today's purported goal was not met. I did not bag fifty-one species, even figuratively. Not every tree keeps its supply of detached leaves tucked below. Some, like yellow buckeye, had been blown clear, all evidence gone. Some I didn't lay eyes on, what with skipping the last leg of the trail. Dawdling so long at each specimen had shifted the balance from inquisitive and lazy to hot and hungry, and then to the nearest drive-through french fries.

The truth is, I'm not lazy. Anxious people rarely are. I take a long time to go a short way when I have the luxury of a tree map, a hand lens, and a couple of hours of solitude in a well-planned meadow. This was my own field trip, teacher and student. I needed time to introduce myself to the nature so obligingly at hand, to see—really see—signs of the season, which today were leaving fast.

Animal, Vegetable, Mineral

At the Agricultural Festival, in the barn with "10,000 specimens of butterflies, moths, bees, flies, spiders, and beetles," a twenty-something couple corners the educator near the "miscellaneous" case. When I overhear "brown marmorated stink bug"—an exotic agricultural pest—I creep closer. Girlfriend keeps quiet, but Dude, whose hand is tucked in the back pocket of Girlfriend's shorts, asks, "How do you kill it?"

"Well," the educator says, "we try to use biological methods to combat insect pests rather than pesticides. We might find another animal that likes to eat this one."

"Animal? You mean bug."

"Insects are animals."

"Insects are animals?"

"On this earth, you are an animal, vegetable, or mineral. Insects are in the animal kingdom."

Dude shakes head. "You learn something new every day."

Stinko Ginkgo

On my walk from the gym's warm water therapy pool—or locally, the *ar-thur-eye-tis* pool—I looted the ginkgo again. It was high autumn, and ginkgo leaves were shifting from green to gold. This time I knew better than to pocket the fallen fruit or drop it into my purse. This time I held a few in my flat palm on the way to the car, where I tipped them into a bag on the floorboard. Last year my coat and purse reeked for days. Blame it on butyric acid. Some say the stench is reminiscent of artisanal cheese, some say vomit or dog poo. Each is accurate.

I hear about people foraging ginkgoes in cities, but I never see them. The foragers, I mean. I see the ginkgoes fine. Then again, I forage on a busy street and no one sees me at it. I am invisible as I squat, hoping my jeans don't flash a plumber's crack, hoping someone will walk near (but not from behind) and ask what I'm doing so I can tell them— tell *someone*—and they will be at least slightly interested.

Also, this time I fiddled with the fruit in my driveway, not my unventilated kitchen. And I wore Playtex gloves to protect against the stink. Against the itch too: the pulp contains an allergen too close to poison ivy to risk the rash.

Each kernel shot from its toxic plum with a squeeze, and I walked the waste straight to the compost pile. I rinsed the hulls and boiled them in salty water for about half an hour.

Should I have cracked the hulls before boiling? One problem with ginkgo tutorials is that most deal with store-bought seeds, not spoils fresh from a sidewalk.

Another problem is that there should not be any ginkgo fruit on any sidewalk, but especially this sidewalk at the door of a medical gym, which is also directly opposite the children's hospital and half a block from the grown-up emergency room. Vomit-scented grenades are inappropriate here, if not redundant. Lobby floors do not need puke purée tracked in on shoes.

On the one hand, ginkgo is a traditional Chinese medicine plant and the seeds, in moderation, are nutritious. Ginkgo might cure what made you join a medical gym in the first place. Leaf extracts are believed to help blood flow, memory, fatigue, and *ar-thur-eye-tis*, all of which would be welcomed by my fellow PT water-walkers, some of whom are twenty years past retirement.

On the other hand, the smell might kill you.

Nobody plants a female ginkgo on purpose. The landscapers either didn't know or care or the nursery goofed. This "living fossil" is a species unchanged since the Cretaceous period, but the only way to sex a sapling is to wait until it blooms (in fifteen to twenty-five years) or run biomolecular analysis. And even then a branch or two or more might suddenly offer flowers of the opposite sex. Life finds a way.

The stench of ginkgo fruit is an up-our-nose reminder that plants reproduce to suit themselves and not us. Gardening forums are full of rants about sweetgum balls or walnut hulls or locust pods or Osage oranges or even little bitty hackberry fruits littering a pristine lawn, and none of these even smell bad. But a rogue stinko ginkgo in a carefully maintained hospital landscape? I cherish the irony.

My tiny harvest yielded palatable results. Not delicious but edible and rather pretty, the texture and color like green jelly beans. Next time I might crack and then boil. Will there be a next time? Will I go to the trouble?

At first my goal was to explore an exotic species and to use and appreciate a windfall literally underfoot. It's a thrill to forage without taking one step out of my way, especially when foraged goods are assumed to be not good—not perceived as food at all.

And then I fantasized that I could produce something tasty enough to share and to shock. What if I delivered a cute little cup of ginkgo kernels to the ladies who staff the gym's front desk? What if I astonished them with ambrosial innards of the smelly yuck outside their door?

What? You can eat that garbage? Brenda, get over here and see this!

But my fear was that Brenda and company had not noticed the yuck. Or smelled the smell. Or seen the tree. My fear was that they wouldn't know ginkgo, and wouldn't care.

Things did not go well when I mentioned the tree to two swimmers and a lifeguard. One had never heard the word "ginkgo" before; one changed the subject; one said "really," but not as a question. None had noticed our ginkgo, though they walk under it five days a week.

Is it important that we see what's around us, what grows here? I am happier in the pool when I look up and see green blurs of lacebark elms across the street, the tulip poplar against the window, the ginkgo hard by. This is after I park my car under the willow oak that I watch bloom, leaf, fruit, unleaf. And after I walk past the red maple—red buds, red flowers, red petioles, red samaras, red fall leaves; after I pass the sick sugar maple that sails bark down the storm sewer. They track the seasons. They root me.

Some folks don't look around much. Or take deep sniffs when walking under a golden tree with leaves that flutter like fine-waled fans. Some don't know they are under a tree.

Then again, some people don't actually know the names of front desk ladies—I invented Brenda—because some folks have the social skills of a pool noodle. I know the name of every street tree, but at the gym, I just smile hello to the lobby at large and then trot upstairs to the lockers. This is an irony I do not cherish.

Not seeing trees, not knowing people—maybe ginkgo could help cure these kinds of *eye-tis*, too? Another try could give me a year to work trees into conversations with people whose names I should learn.

≈

But I wouldn't get a year.

A few months later, I walked as usual to the pool at opening time: past the willow oak, the sugar maple, the red maple, the tulip poplar, but this time not past the ginkgo. Past a fresh stump.

"The ginkgo is gone," I wailed to two gym staffers as soon as I'd pushed through the door. Then I clarified, in case they didn't know ginkgo, "The ginkgo tree is gone!"

"Oh, I *know*," the woman at the desk said, wide-eyed. "They cut it down yesterday."

She said she'd gotten an email that the tree was a pedestrian hazard and would be replaced with another kind of tree, presumably less hazardous. Then she read the email to me because I asked, and because she was kind.

"It had such pretty leaves," she said, and sighed.

"I am so sad," the manager added, joining us, making three mourners in the quiet lobby at dawn. "I've been working here for twenty years," she said. "And you know what? My girls played on that tree when they were little."

Early the next wet morning, after a night of the soaking rain I'd waited for, I brought two coffee cups of potting soil in my bag. At the stump I braced my feet in sawdust, reached over the retaining wall and gently, so gently, tugged two ginkgo babies free. They were six inches tall. One still wore its empty fruit skin at soil level. Both were waving tiny, ribbed, fan-shaped leaves, but in secret: low, hidden in mats of wintercreeper, proof that life had found a way.

At six-thirty a.m. I walked the surprise gifts inside. Instead of cute little cups of ginkgo kernels, they were cute little cups of ginkgo trees: one for Shawna at the front desk and one for Karen, the manager. Some folks whose names I learned.

"Little Things That Run the World" in Late October

Let me say a word on behalf of these little
things that run the world.

EDWARD O. WILSON

Just like that: it's time to find the sweatshirts, the coconut
oil is white again, bath towels stay wet, and I want to wear
socks to bed.

Just like that: goldfinches are toppling sunflowers, black-
eyed Susans are *only* black eyes, car wheels pop acorns, and
bees sleep late in the goldenrod.

Just like that: a new neighbor hired Mosquito Joe.

Michael is with me on a walk when we see the mosquito
man with a gas-powered fogger that shoots pesticide at 295
feet a second. We turn to walk a different route until the
spray can settle on trees and bushes and grass and flowers,
and on bees and caterpillars and ladybugs and soldier beetles and jumping spiders and butterflies that had been there
one second ago; 295 feet ago; little things doing their thing:
eating, getting eaten, keeping our world running.

Just like that.

Nature's Motel

Numerous picnic shelters in both Percy and
Edwin Warner Parks have invited visitors to
gather since their construction in the 1930s.
During the New Deal, the Works Progress
Administration hired craftsmen to build the
shelters with limestone and cedar found right
here in the Parks and surrounding area.

FRIENDS OF WARNER PARKS

"What's a drug deal?" Izzy asked on our dog walk this
morning. He is nine. He had overheard us talking about
maybe going back to Indian Springs.

We go back.

Indian Springs is a beauty spot at Warner Parks in Nashville. As a dead end, it feels remote though it isn't. It feels
susceptible to assignations, which it is. In baby Maggie
days—twenty-plus years ago—we'd take a picnic or a Frisbee but cautiously, knowing we might need to shift to Beech
Grove if things didn't feel right. Back then the shelters at
Indian Springs were iffy, as were the occasional cars that
eased through—none of which looked outdoorsy (make/
model/year, no charity license plate or sporty bumper

sticker), and none of which contained more than a driver. He (always a he) neither looked nor waved and didn't even lift the index finger draped atop the steering wheel, which everyone knows is the official minimum.

The lane is on the left as Beech Grove comes into view. It rises then falls around a wooded hill toward a little turn-around with an old slippery elm as hub. Three recently re-stored award-winning shelters radiate from the elm: shelter 2 on the left, shelter 3 in front, and shelter 4 on the right, after the lane elbows through elm, persimmon, hackberry, beech, sycamore, and walnut. Shelter 4, which is hidden from the hub when trees are in leaf, is where I'd schedule my drug deals, no question. Shelter 1 is so small you might not notice it on your way in. It's a covered picnic table beside the lane, but nicely done.

It is two days before Halloween, sunny and hot, and I have a migraine. Migraines magnify sunny and hot. They magnify smells too, so it's a good thing I like the smell of walnut, because we climb out of my car (visibly outdoorsy) into a wall of walnut perfume. The lane is cobbled with outer hulls and inner shells in every stage of round to flat, and in all possible walnut colors, greens, yellows, browns and blacks, with accent whites of meat not yet stained. Hun-dreds of freshly fallen, still intact walnuts—the fattest hulls I have ever seen—have pooled themselves into dips in the verge and rolled toward the drainage ditch. We hear the *chonk* of a walnut hitting the grass from high overhead and know better than to stand too close.

A car comes down the drive. Old car, no wave; circles the elm and drives out.

Have you picked up a walnut fresh from a tree and sniffed it? Have you dug your fingernails into the soft leather and sniffed again? Or rubbed the green leaves or snapped a twig? They are marvelous smells, and all the same chemical: juglone. A bit lemony, some say, but deeper and browner and walnuttier. If you are the mani-pedi type, skip the fingernail test, because juglone is a dye so durable it needs no mordant, even when you dip your duvet cover into a half-whiskey barrel of a few hulls swilled with water from the garden hose. The skin under your nails will be walnut-colored for weeks. Your duvet cover will be walnut-colored forever.

Juglone is more than a dye; it is chemical warfare. When released into the soil by roots, leaves, or fallen fruit, it can inhibit the germination and growth of a long list of plants. The word is allelopathy: "of each another" plus "suffer." I looked it up, and the word was first used in 1938, roughly around the time these shelters were constructed. Not all plants are susceptible to juglone (hackberries do not care), but you wouldn't want to put a tomato garden near the drip line. Or peppers or eggplants. I found this out when I was planning raised beds at school, where our parking lot is anchored by the walnut tree donor of my duvet dye.

We are at Indian Springs to scout a good site for Michael's birthday party. His fortieth was at a shelter by the Little Harpeth River, as was Maggie's tenth. Both were muddy bliss. The park's Friends group has restored all the historic Works Progress Administration shelters, and they are gorgeous: post-framed with unpeeled cedar and fat, creamy, squared columns still wearing scars from the mill. Inside, look up to see saplings radiate tight and shaggy from the ridgepole.

Shelter 2 is in front of our car, but we start with shelter 3—wide, bright, room for a party—and then walk toward shelter 4. Another car comes, turns around, and leaves. I should look at these cars, but I can't. I should note details for the crime report. No, I should look to assess the actual situation and not the ones in my imagination.

A big beech to the right of the lane has been graffitied nearly to death. Beech never outgrows its smooth gray bark, and for time beyond record the genus has invited inscription. I've read that the words "beech" and "book" share a common root, as if beech trees were our first books, but not everyone agrees.

This tree is pure palimpsest up to about eight feet off the ground, with new and old and older tokens merging. The highest design puzzles me at first. Surely they'd have needed a ladder? Then I remember that it is possible if not advisable to stand on the roof of a pickup truck. Most hearts and initials have swollen and merged beyond legibility, but some gouges are an inch deep. One reads "1956." A heart floating alone, clear as a cattle brand, reads "Angela + Kevin."

Once a tree is girdled, and this one looks girdled, it will die. A tree lives under the bark in the cambium layer, and if wounds cinch the trunk there are no more pathways to deliver and receive water and food. Warner Park naturalists mention this on guided walks when they stand next to big beeches, and I'm glad they do because I doubt a single inscriber knew they were killing a tree with a moment's work of a jackknife.

The naturalists call beech trees "nature's motels." This phrase usually elicits a titter, which I'm also glad about. It means listeners might remember that beech trees alive or dead can shelter countless creatures, from bacteria and fungi to birds and mammals. No one removes dead trees here, and snags are left standing. At Warner there is always room at the inn.

Another car comes, goes. I can't tell which poppings under slow tires are gravel and which are walnuts.

And here's where I need to talk about the botanical genus of walnuts: *Juglans*. The khaki-colored, wrinkled walnut shells at the grocery store are *Juglans regia*, the royal walnut, aka English and Persian walnut. Our walnuts in the park are a native American, *Juglans nigra*, or black walnut. They are not at the grocery store, and they are harder to husk and crack and nearly impossible to clean of meat, but they are worth it.

It's the name *Juglans* that interests me, especially today at Indian Springs. It's what the compound juglone is named after. *Juglans* is most often translated as Jupiter's nut, as in a nut fit not only for gods but for the biggest god. Linneus, the namer, had a sense of humor: Ju-glans meant Jupiter's glans, as in Jupiter's *glans*. As in sixth-grade sex education. Actually, I would have thought Jupiter's *testis* more appropriate, given the creased, lobed spheres of any walnut shell.

Then again, g*lans* also means acorn in Latin, and it can refer to the tree fruits of oak, beech, chestnut, date, and cashew. It makes sense that Jupiter's acorns—walnuts—would be bigger than mere mortal, um, acorns. But my point is that walnuts are a dirty joke, and today we can hardly take a step without tripping over dirty jokes. Dirty jokes are falling from the sky.

The bright lane is a relief to rejoin. Izzy and I pick up fallen slippery elm leaves longer than our palms. They are scratchy on top and underneath.

"That's dumb," he says. "Why doesn't slippery elm have slippery leaves?"

The inner bark is what's slippery, but we don't want to hurt a tree to prove it.

Twenty years ago I knew slippery elm as a throat lozenge, not a tree in my own city. I have photos of the three of us at Indian Springs—Michael, Maggie, and me—and see not one baby but three, which is ridiculous as two of us were at least thirty at the time. We look young, hairy, happy, and utterly bound to one another, complete. That summer day Michael stretched Maggie to the lowest limb of that elm by the hub, and I took a picture. Then he sat her upright in the sloping field and we ran away, took a picture, ran farther, took another, ran farther, until she was a pink dot in the green grass, sitting, waiting, watching with those heavylidded, cow-dark eyes.

The limb where she sat has been sawed off, but the scarred old beech beside the elm is still there. The beech is hollow but still alive: nature's motel.

Here we separate. Izzy prefers to kick walnuts down and across and up the gravel, so we leave him behind to go try shelter 2. He is in sun and in view and I pretend I am not the least worried that another car has come while we were rubbing leaves and that the distance between us grows, like I pretended with the dot of Maggie in the grass. This car is parked close to mine, so close that we wonder if we will be able to get back in without hitting a door. This is weird, because there are yards and yards of room, of road, of grass. The person, one man, is up at the shelter we had not yet seen. Bummer. We've missed our chance to get a feel for it. And I've missed my chance to show Izzy the hollow beech, because it is too close to the man's car and directly under the shelter. The vibe has changed.

Another car (not outdoorsy) drives up and parks. A woman gets out and lopes directly at our dog.

"Hello, girl!" She knew Bea was female without bending to look. "Hellooo, girrrrull! What's your name?"

"Beatrice," Michael answers. I stare.

"Bee-a-trice! Do you call her Bea? Or Beatrice?"

"We call her everything."

"Everything!? Nooo, honey, you can't let Daddy and Momma call you everything!" She squats in her tiny terry stretch shorts and tight white camisole and loves on our dog *hard*. She grabs her and hugs her and rakes her fur backward and pats and slaps, and kisses her head. Beatrice looks at Michael for a clue what to do.

"What kind of dog is she?" the woman says. Which leads to our prepared statement about how we only know that the mom was a border collie but we think the father was another shepherd and how she likes to herd us.

Pretty lady has a dog too, she says, and her dog is part shepherd too.

Her skin is smooth. Her face, those thighs, everywhere, and all the same creamy beige. How is skin ever that smooth on an adult? I could not guess her age if my life depended on it.

"Well, bye!" we say, and turn to walk down the drive, Michael toward flinty rocks by the wooden bridge, me toward more walnut trees. The walnut hulls are as big as baseballs. Massive. Fertile. Juicy. The god of nuts.

"Bea! Bea!" The woman is still there, now hollering. She whistles. Beatrice looks at her but does not go.

By now my migraine is swelling from the sun and the heat and the weirdness with the cars and that woman, and I am pulled by the shade of the covered picnic table at shelter 1 to sit and admire Izzy from afar. He is still scissor-kicking walnuts on the lane.

A car leaves. What car? I don't remember seeing it enter, and I pretend not to see it leave. It's too personal here, too close, like standing in an elevator with strangers. There is an etiquette at Indian Springs, and it includes not looking pointedly at cars.

That's when I hear it. About five minutes after the woman whistles for Beatrice, I start hearing noises. His, hers. Rhythmic. Moan-gasp-screams. Loud. Oh, good god almighty. By Jupiter's beard and by Jove, the pretty lady and the car man are in shelter 2 and they are full on at it. I should mention that the shelter has a back wall for the fireplace and chimney, but three sides are open to the road. These shelters reveal the onboard picnic tables and whatever might be happening onboard those tables.

It is eleven-thirty on a Saturday morning.

And, look, here are more people arriving but on foot: a conventional-looking couple (outdoorsy) walking up the drive toward the shelters, talking, not yet making meaning from the groans and screams that must be reaching them by now. I call to Michael and he walks to me and hears what I hear and we look at each other and we both say it is time to go.

One more thing about walnut trees. The fruit are juglone bombs. Throwing walnuts in a pond (or setting a sackful in a river) is an efficient but illegal way to stun and kill fish. I learned about this after a friend innocently placed her kids' tadpole tub under a walnut tree. I also learned that some fishermen pour walnut water on the ground to force night-crawlers up toward a waiting bucket, because walnut water costs nothing and chlorine bleach does.

If the couple in shelter 2 is walnut water, we are the worms.

I yell for Izzy. As we all get to the car, I wonder aloud about lunch to divert him from looking up at the man in the shelter with his back to us and the smooth lady riding his lap. I think of her terry shorts, how my friends and I used to wear shorts like that in middle school and how—not that any of us dreamed of such a thing then—those shorts could so easily be slipped down and off in about two seconds, or if time did not permit that, how the polycotton crotch could stretch to the side and stay there a while, allowing unhindered access to areas required.

I think also that when we do find the right birthday shelter, I'll bring disinfectant.

Later Michael and I agree that (1) she was on something, because no grownup is that happy to see a dog, and (2) this was likely a commercial transaction: the arrival at different times and the curious combination of delay (the time she took with our dog) and speed (the time it took to start moaning). I suspect that the customer prefers a public transaction; this spot meets the requirement, and at a fairly low risk of police interference. In other words, this was not "Angela + Kevin."

Tonight, still with a migraine, I clock through the rituals of Izzy's bedtime. I choose *The Hidden Life of Trees* to bore him to sleep—all nature books are soporifics—and come upon the page about an old beech with the heartwood gone. It is alive: hollow but strong for now, like a pipe. The business of living, as in all trees, is carried out in the walls of the pipe—the cambium I mentioned (where water and food travel) and the sapwood next to it (where energy is stored). And I thought about the old beech by our car at Indian Springs and how I had been drawn to it as soon as I emerged into the walnut fug. How it wasn't completely girdled like the graffitied one nearby. How it was hollow and how the front, facing us, had a wide, wavy opening from the ground up like a good-sized door, rather like Piglet's beech house in *Winnie the Pooh*. How there was a little window in the back wall of our tree, so that from the wavy door I could see through the tree to the shelter behind: the shelter where the couple would be having noisy seated sex half an hour later. And I couldn't help but think about today's missing heartwood in the drama of Indian Springs, the holes, the pipe—and Jupiter's big nuts simply everywhere—and the business of living being carried on by the outer layer, the part that holds everything up.

And, too, the absolute vindication of my imagined code of etiquette at Indian Springs.

I close my book and realize that I had stopped reading aloud a while ago. Izzy has been asleep since the first paragraph. I watch him breathing at my elbow and see tumbled on the floor walnut-stained sneakers half a size smaller than mine. I am grateful for this heartwood and sapwood and cambium and bark and leaves and roots right here, right now.

And I know next time I hear the phrase "nature's motel" on a public hike, I will have a story to share but won't.

Evidence

My pockets tell me when I've had the best days. They burp catalpa seeds, surrender snail shells, turn out twigs of spicebush, fumble oak apples round and dry.

Sometimes blue jeans keep a leaf I don't find until after the dryer cycle, and once I forgot a stub of charcoal from a prairie burn, but it caught in that little offset pocket, that vestigial nod to pocket watches (though the Levi's blog mentions tickets, coins, and condoms), and it only made marks on the inside.

To make marks is an art class thing I have always loved: simple language for simple gesture and complicated need. We make marks to give voice; to record something, anything; to *make our mark*, because treasures can't keep in pockets for long.

White Pine Smells Mighty Fine

It's hard to be a tree in a city. People plant you under power lines, mulch you to death, pour asphalt up to your trunk, cut your head off. People smother your drip line with weed barrier. People spray you with poison to kill "bugs," or inject you with it, so murder creeps up your innards to wait in every leaf, every grain of pollen, every drop of sap. People hate when you drop all the things trees are meant to drop: leaves, twigs, flowers, seeds, fruit. And then the dropped things are not allowed to stay, although the plan was to rot into rich food for your roots.

White pine is a favorite because it was a first and because, if pronounced with a Knoxville accent, the twin vowels sound like home.

Say it with me. Take the i of white and pine, eliminate the diphthong, then stretch your mouth into a short shallow a. The closest phonetic notation is æ. Make sure to widen it right out the front of your face: *whæt pæn*.

Next say a sentence that happens to be true: White pine

smells mighty fine. Make the vowels match. You will sound like a native.

As a bonus, this same vowel is a diagnostic tool for species identification. Pine needles happen in bundles, and each species packs a particular number of needles per bundle. How many needles in white pine? *Fæve*. Check a twig and count: one, two, three, four, *fæve*.

I'm learning the cycle of our neighbor Emmaly's white pine. There's a branch in our yard, easy to see. It fell, so I dragged it from her lawn and up our driveway and dropped it where I would smell the mighty fine from my bat-watch chair. It took a while at the sink later, with lye soap and hot water, to scrub the resin off my hands. Which reminded me of Knoxville, because that stickiness, like the red clay where it grew, was impossible to get out of clothes.

Resin, for the record, is drooled sap, and rosin is resin worked into something serviceable, like what's powdered in a bag on a pitcher's mound or what a fiddler uses to "rosin up the bow."

When I was a child there was a restaurant that still served potatoes, whole, cooked in rosin. But how could anyone gather enough rosin to fill a pot? What must the kitchen smell like with pinesap bubbling on the stove? And how did it not catch fire? Dad said his grandmother "Maw used to boil potatoes in rosin." So I ordered one once, hungry to eat my heritage and to taste what is usually perfume. But it was just a baked potato. Why bother with rosin if the result might as well have come out of a microwave? I suspect the menu of embroidery. It was Cracker Barrel—no surprise— which excels at Olde Tyme nostalgic white people fantasies. Maybe rosin was one of them.

In spring male white pine flowers shed pollen. With a poke from a finger, a cloud of yellow dust explodes into the breeze. Serious foragers collect pine pollen for cooking, and I should at least lick my hand, but I keep forgetting. Female flowers are too high to see without binoculars.

This is the only native pine I've seen at our sidewalks, except for the fence-line trees at the gated community. Most conifers are from up north or another continent. Although I wish creatures in the hood had more native food and cover in winter, I get why folks aren't rushing to buy trees that grow 150 feet tall. In America's virgin forests, white pines grew much taller, and made the most valuable ship masts in the world. Some say the Revolutionary War was as much about white pine as it was about tea; colonists didn't like the Royal Navy taking the best trees for free.

This fall I noticed that Emmaly's pine looked poorly. It never looks good, because for years Nashville Electric Service has scraped it into a monster. They call it "side pruning," where the street side is shaved bare while the other sides bristle in compensation. And they call the top chop "overhang removal," where fifteen feet above a power line is hacked clear of lateral branches.

Despite tortured pruning, the tree survives. Crows nest

in a top so high it towers over rooflines blocks away. Every year the tree donates cones for kindergarten bird feeders at our school. But when I looked last month, half the tree was sprinkled with rust, as if handfuls of needles were okay and handfuls were not. Oh no, I thought. It's finally dying.

A week later the tree was green. Underneath were hills of pine straw, as if Mr. Bee, who mows Emmaly's yard, had dumped a bale but forgotten to rake. That's when I realized the tree had a plan. It's called a shed cycle.

As kids we learn that there are two kinds of trees: deciduous and evergreen. "Evergreens are ever green and never lose their leaves." But nothing is this simple. All evergreens lose leaves, but usually not in one go. Only fake Christmas trees are green forever.

About a third of the needles die each year on a white pine, so for a while a tree can look worrisome. But down they come as planned, the dead needles, and I take them, a few to stuff in flowerpots, fling onto the garden, and hold to my face with both hands and breathe.

Emmaly is relaxed about yard care, unlike new people who buy renovated homes and expect renovated landscaping. She probably hasn't noticed her rusty branches, and even if she had she would put off calling a tree guy long enough to notice she didn't need a tree guy. But if, say, Party House down the street had a white pine that went brown, he wouldn't wait. Then again, he wouldn't tolerate a deformed tree in the first place. He took out a hackberry, a black locust, and an elm just to free up space for guest parking.

The neighborhood is louder than usual with chain saws. Next Door cut down a big hackberry to make room for concrete pavers. Another neighbor took out two hackberries that anchored a corner of my sky.

People like the idea of trees, but the realities are complicated. Maybe we would be better off planting fake Christmas trees.

The couple who bought Mutant Renovation House lost a sugar maple and two red oaks, all of which they unwittingly drowned with an overly ambitious irrigation system. I imagine they thought the existing privet, nandina, burning bush, bamboo, English ivy, and euonymus needed pampering. Bless them. You can't kill those invasive pests even if you try.

In the essay "Pines above the Snow," which would have told me about shed cycles had I read it earlier, Aldo Leopold calls fallen pine needles "accumulated wisdom."

After Emmaly's pine needles fell, and after I stole my handful, I happened to look out the window. Mr. Bee was underneath the tree doing what he must have done these past twenty-something autumns when I wasn't looking. He was transferring new rusty clumps—the mighty fine pine straw, the same stuff I buy by the bale at Hillsboro Hardware, the "accumulated wisdom"—into plastic bags for the trash.

There's a Yiddish saying, "Mann traoch, Gott Lauch," or

"Man plans, God laughs." Its origin is in Psalms. Here's my variation: "Trees plan, Man laughs." Its origin is in every city tree.

Sometimes trees laugh.

You know that gated community I mentioned, ringed with white pine? The trees were planted as a privacy screen, to hide chain-link fencing and the huge homes that sit behind it, and to hide patios from passersby.

What I didn't mention was that white pine grows branches in whorls, one whorl a year, and as the tree rises the lowest whorls drop. Mature trees have no branches for a long way from ground to crown. This was one characteristic that made white pine so valuable as masts for ships. But the same characteristic makes white pine less than ideal for privacy screens.

When I pass the gated patios, I see patios. I see state-of-the-art gas grills and outdoor kitchens, I see deck umbrellas, I see artisan-crafted kid forts. And I laugh. Man plans, woman laughs.

I don't know if the white pines laugh, but they do smell mighty fine.

Compression

En route to another mammogram, I stop at a catalpa tree. It's at the office building on Music Row with twin northern catalpas in a corner. I have to pee pretty bad and could use a Pepcid pronto, but first I need November leaves. I don't pluck, because trees feel, which I've always known but science now proves, so I hunt wet grass for yellowed hearts bigger than my hand, bigger than the book I brought for the wait—leaves not yet stiffened into crackling brown, leaves still velvet underneath, leaves I soon realize won't fit in my 8.5 × 11 notebook without spearing past the covers.

When I get to the hospital I bring the leaves—all but one—to the waiting room, which isn't a room but the sla- lomed aisle of a shopping mall that forty-one years ago was such a big deal my family drove three hours on the inter- state to see it.

And when I check in I wonder if the woman behind the counter—and every person of every color down this longer- than-a-football-field hallway—I wonder if they assume that my white, middle-aged, middle-class, straight, mar- ried female southern self voted for the racist, misogynist, homophobic, narcissistic, and staggeringly unqualified cli-

mate change denier who won the presidential election in
the wee hours of this very morning.

And when I wait for my name, I smooth the soft leaves,
press them one at a time, pull each between pages of my
notebook, pat the velvet, trace the scars, finger veins to the
margins, and mash them flat, flat to dry flat.

And when I drop my borrowed robe, I let a machine do
something similar to my body, but with clamps and radia-
tion and pain: press soft breasts one at a time, pull each between pages of polycarbonate, tug the skin, shift the nipple,
stretch the flesh and mash flat, flat, to capture, to assess if I
must come back tomorrow for biopsies or in six months for
another go. To see what, if anything, science can prove.

And later, hours later, when I get in the car to drive my
boy to Hebrew school, I put my tote bag on the floorboard
and hear the one leaf I'd left behind: the enormous, golden,
smooth and slide-y heart I did not bring in to the hospital
because I was afraid to harm what would have flopped from
three sides of my notebook. Sun has curled and puckered
and ridged it like 4-H tobacco at the state fair. Except for the
bit under my bag, which is what I heard, and which is now
freed in brittle flakes as flat as flat can be.

Eponymous

Mount View Glade is nine acres of state natural area bound by road and residential subdivision. From anywhere inside this sliver—this piece of pie left to stand for the whole—a visitor can see or hear cars and houses, especially after autumn leaf-fall.

In 1968 this is where Elsie Quarterman found the Tennessee coneflower (*Echinacea tennesseensis*), presumed extinct. It's still here, thanks to her and her student minions, saved with such vigor that it was bumped from the federal endangered list in 2011. I love how it pops up in the drainage ditch across the street. Last year we saw a homeowner shave it from his mailbox with a weed eater.

If you haven't seen Tennessee coneflower, I'd tell you to imagine a child's drawing of a purply pink daisy but with narrow petals cocked forward to hug the viewer. The middle—the cone—is a prickly dome of interlocking swirls in greenish bronze, sometimes with the tiniest blip of yellow pollen spiked atop an outer row. The stems are adorably hairy. I'd tell you that each flower faces roughly east-southeast (we check with a compass) and does not, as you might expect, chase the sun across open-skied glade.

To see it properly, come in June and walk a moment through scruffy brush, past cedars and infant oaks to the clearing—the glade, the "wasteland"—and there it'll be, spearing up from limestone gravel as if sown like a crop.

We went today, but in late November coneflowers look like weeds, reduced to prickly seed heads: cones on a stick. I molested a single seed out of its puzzle and nibbled it. My mouth needed a reminder of how Tennessee coneflower tastes.

Oh, hell.

A botanist once told me the zinc content is what makes my tongue feel like I've licked a battery, but I don't know for sure. Folks don't seem to go around chewing *E. tennesseensis* and analyzing the data.

Mount View is named for the road, which so far has exhibited neither mount nor view. Still, we drive from Nashville for the tiny view in the glade and to do our bit and pick up trash. We plucked plastic from reindeer lichen, a Funyuns bag from glade moss. There were Coke cups, Red Bull cans, and one heavy McDonald's sack I did not open, but all the trash is from the road, from the outside in, not from picnics or assignations inside. There is no room for secrecy here. And unlike at larger glades, we never find bullet casings or lead shot. This place is too small to shoot anything without hitting everything.

The boys wandered, Michael looking down at fossils, Izzy whomping bush honeysuckle with a stick. I found two lanceleaf gumweed flowers still yellow. These plants are so tough I've seen them bloom through a bona fide drought, with the eponymous bead of gum still inside like a single sparkly dewdrop. Cedar glades in summer are always droughty with so little soil to hold moisture, but a few summers ago they fried. Not to death. Dry can't kill a cedar glade. Only people can.

The funny thing is that sometimes glade land looks like it's already dead. A lot of it is rock. Great stretches could be an abandoned parking lot or a demolition site, but what you think must be old concrete is limestone a lot older—about 460 million years older—with every chunk, big or small, pebbled with bodies of sea creatures and sculpted by rain.

You'd be surprised what can grow on bare rock, what can shimmy from cracks, what can root in eddies between shatters of gravel. A mosaic of lichen, liverwort, moss, nostoc, sedum, prickly pear. Native grass and sedge are November seas of khaki and copper. Against these subtle strata, showy flowers are a bonus. Something blooms here nearly every month, even if you have to hunt to find it. Glade cress can start at the end of January with white and pink and yellow blooms underfoot in the clackety grit. Three colors but one species, all smelling like honey—good local honey with notes of clover.

Dr. Quarterman carved glade complexes into zones based on depth of soil, starting with zone 1 with no soil at all and progressing to zone 6 with the twelve inches that can support mature oak and hickory. Each zone, along with its margin, grows particular plants and supports particular species. Not particular is the eastern red cedar (*Juniperus virginiana*). I'm calling it meta-zonal, although I can't find the word in dictionaries. Cedar ubiquity names its own haven: the eponymous cedar glade. Teachers will tell you a more accurate term is "limestone glade," but cedars will win.

Mount View is so small that it barely makes it to the deep stuff. But it's a glade: a globally rare ecosystem full of wonders—including endemic species like our Tennessee coneflower—and in need of protection. All glades are islands now, ringed by development.

It used to be that no one could build on glade land, not in a big way. Put in trailer homes, yes, but not proper residential or business real estate. Because of the rock. When someone figured out how to build septic systems on exposed bedrock and atop infamously unstable karst topography, the game changed. In cedar glades you stand on fissures and caves, underground streams and sinkholes layered in limestone still eroding with each rain. I've been told that new subdivisions have to set aside a parcel every now and then and hold back a numbered lot from sale. Why? A sinkhole, awakened by bulldozers.

The coneflower is what saved this little glade. It is a photogenic plant, a proper poster flower to charm the public. It's a flower you'd want to buy in gallon pots at Walmart. I wonder how big the glade used to be, before development. The hypotenuse of Mount View's triangle is Coneflower Trail, a new short dead-end street. Aerial views show fresh homes tucked tight in kelly green rectangles of sod, and room for maybe twelve more lots, barring sinkholes.

Do Coneflower Trail homeowners know about coneflowers? Do they know the street destroyed trails? Do they know their own houses displace that many square feet of rare ecosystem? Do they know that a weed-'n'-feed lawn will never grow glade cress or Nashville breadroot or Tennessee milk vetch or gumweed or even the poster flower the street is named for? The coneflower isn't endangered any more, but its habitat is. Not that I blame the residents. They bought land and a tract home fair and square. But I'm glad someone had foresight and grit and budget enough to fence this triangle from its fate as yet another garage-centric, chimneyless, cookie-cutter development.

A hundred feet from Coneflower Trail today, Izzy cracked a fallen cedar limb. Michael passed it to me to sniff, as usual. That smell. A spicy, warm, resinous tang. Love is too pale a word. The bark was pale though, bleached the same gray as the limestone from where it grew, but the inside split was shocking: bright pink, fuchsia, orange in banded waves. Does each color have its own smell?

Aside from cedar needles, almost everything else green at Mount View this time of year is bush honeysuckle, English ivy, and privet. These garden escapees slowly shade and strangle native plants that make a glade a glade. A Weed Wrangle would require volunteer teams with uprooters and good backs.

We are a volunteer team with grocery bags, and only one of us has a back I'd call good. Nothing can keep out bush honeysuckle.

Someone, sometime, tried to keep out something here. We were curious about the remains of a low stone wall. It starts from bare earth with the hint of berm and leads to the old road. So much rock must have taken weeks to collect and stack, but even at its full height the wall couldn't have been more than two feet tall tops. There were six-foot cedar posts—not trees but anchored, sawed lengths from trees— four feet apart at the berm end. Why? Were they posts for a gate? The mystery was a nice distraction from the after-shocks of that one coneflower seed. My mouth still tasted of old pennies.

The Tennessee Department of Environment and Con-servation description says the land used to be heavily grazed, but I can't see that piddly wall ever keeping a grazer in or out. There must have been barbed wire, removed when the Nature Conservancy rescued this slice of pie in 1990 or later, when TDEC took over, or whenever the visitor loop was created. Barbed wire—new and vintage—is a common denominator of every state-owned cedar glade we visit. Posts and wire are part of the history of use, a clue to how the land has been called to function by owners: as a trash dump, hunting ground, or, in areas with enough dirt to hold grass, thin pasture. The newest wire at Mount View backs backyards of the suburban dead end.

It cuts Coneflower Trail from the coneflower trail.

People still throw trash in cedar glades and still shoot if there's room, but nothing grazes at Mount View except small wild things that can't be held by fences: turkey, squir-rel, songbirds, boys with sticks, nerds with fossils, and the odd naturalist who loves the place so much she needs to eat it.

This Is How a Robin Drinks

The birdbath with the most action is accidental. It's just a big plastic saucer forgotten on the driveway but found and filled by storms. The dog loves it, the red wasps love it, and so do robins, doves, and cardinals—birds comfortable on the ground. Between it and me are an old lawn chair and a screened door that act as a bird blind. Birds at the saucer don't see me here on the porch, but I see them fine. They drink alone; they drink together. When they bathe, they splash water on thirsty concrete and then butterflies aim for the dark glittering stains.

There has been no rain for twelve days in a row. Before dawn I walked the yard in flip-flops to stare at the sky—no clouds—and although the grass is overlong, my feet stayed dry. When I came inside for tea, still thinking about stars, I learned that overnight we'd set a new record for the deadliest mass-shooting in US history. More than the usual number of dead and wounded.

I filled the driveway saucer after I took our boy to school. Not knowing what else to do, I sat to watch birds who did. It's fall migration, and birds need what I've got: seeds in the feeder, seeds in the wildflower patch; and for birds who eat fruit or insects, the hackberry tree in our little yard has both. Each fall yellow-green warblers strip it of tiny psyllids and woolly aphids, while robins gorge on berries. And all birds need water, placed high and low. I always wonder what they make of city fluoride and chlorine. Can they taste them? Do they wish I'd draw water from the rain barrel instead?

A robin flew down pretty quick and perched on the edge of the full saucer. He froze, watchful. His white-rimmed eye did not see me. He dipped his head, scooped some water, and lifted his beak to let gravity slide the sip to his gullet. I could see his throat quiver as the muscles worked. No, quiver is too delicate a word. I mean more of a judder, like when my husband turns the hose bibb not quite far enough to the left ("lefty loosey") and the supply pipe judders in the basement so hard it shakes the kitchen floor. The robin's throat looked like this sounds, like it had to hammer that drink down. So much work for a bit of water, but it's how most birds have to do it.

The robin dipped, raised, dipped, raised, again and again. When his beak was in the water, ripples radiated to the edge of the plastic. When his beak was in the air, the surface of the saucer had already stilled. It was as if there was room for only one set of ripples at a time: either the water or the throat. I kept watching both—the taking of turns, the shimmers of wet, the shivers of feather, when would the pattern break? I was afraid to move or blink. I was afraid he would stop drinking, and I was afraid he would never stop drinking. When at last he fluttered up to the hackberry tree in his own good time, I found that I was crying.

There is room for a thing to be astonishing and mundane at the same time. An accidental birdbath. Ripples. A sunlit drop at the tip of a beak. The matching grays of a robin's wing and old concrete. The next peacetime massacre with weapons of war, and the next, and the next, and the next. Watching a robin drink what is offered.

.

Winter

Frost Flowers

"Let's go see the ice mushrooms," Michael said. His tone implied the trip would be worth trading a warm house for a cold drive, but I didn't expect much. I figured he meant *frost heaves*, like when frozen soil burps itself into needled buttes. Heaves happen in the lawn sometimes—they rise an inch or so tall and then crrrunch underfoot in the most satisfying way.

But no, he led us to a long meadow deep in Warner Park with hundreds and hundreds of what I can now call frost flowers: white ice formations abloom from the base of nearly every meadow stem—as wheels, arabesques, bottlebrushes, and especially, miraculously, as *ribbons* snaking through stubble, looping back on themselves in tight slaloms, pretzeling around dead leaves and brambles. The ice was corded, striated—not like grosgrain ribbon on the transverse, but parallel, like that fancy ribbon candy I've never seen anyone actually eat. The tallest stems—up to six feet—wore capes frozen in mid-billow, as formal as a Leonardo drapery study.

When morning sun hit them, they glowed.

These, we do not step on.

Clueless as to the exact cause and certainly clueless as to the species of real flower they sprang from, we marveled, we knelt, we poked, and a few, we licked and bit.

Frost flowers.

Right now, these native "flowers" are blooming in Nashville—at least, until they melt, which is typically right after they form. Frost flowers are winter ephemerals. They happen when air temperature drops below freezing and warm groundwater rises to extrude itself through the conduit of a real flower stem, especially if that stem is a white crownbeard (*Verbesina virginica*). "Ice segregation" is the process at work. Water and vapor freeze on contact with air, and waves from within push older crystals forward and out. Crownbeard's winged structure aids the process. Other species can produce frost flowers, but white crownbeard is such a common enabler that the plant's most common common name is frostweed.

The taller the plant, the taller the ice sculptures. The short stalks I found today had been mown by the city, and illustrate another good reason to put off mowing until spring. Spent flowers left standing can feed seed-eating birds, house overwintering pollinators, give cover for wildlife, *and* make spectacular ice art.

This year I missed the first crop at Warner, which was the November morning after first frost. I missed the next crop in early December because I was home with a sick kid. I was bummed.

And then yesterday, washing dishes and feeling sorry for myself, I remembered my friend Gail had given me a baby white crownbeard last summer. A native aster had piggy-backed in the same pot, and in my ratty garden had grown so much taller and bushier than the crownbeard I'd forgotten about the shorter gift. I ran coatless to the backyard and there it was: my own private frost flower, spinning a curtain between two dried stalks.

I hope my little plant likes my garden. I hope it can seed itself into a flurry, a snow shower, a snowstorm, a blizzard.

Not that white crownbeard is only valuable in winter. It's the larval host plant for several butterflies, and from July to October is a good source of nectar. The true blossoms are small but lovely: rays and discs as white as the stem's winter wings.

I almost missed the mown versions today. On an urgent whim that struck with only an hour until school pickup, I drove to the park in search of leftover ice. There was no time to make it to the long meadow, and besides, sun would have soaked those into the soil by noon. A weedy north-facing lee was my last hope until next winter.

I found them where honey locust pods drop on the road near the Cane Connector trail, at the line where the two Warner parks divide. I stopped the car and reversed, but what I thought were frost flowers was trash: a white Walmart bag, a pair of men's briefs, an empty juice bottle milky white against green-brown grass. They all look like ice sculptures from a moving car.

But there—at the same height as the wads of toilet paper

and sandwich foil—curved dozens of stubby frost flowers, still frozen at two o'clock in the afternoon thanks to the shade of a sugar maple and a berm of privet. The contrast of treasure and trash (and trash shrubs) made me happy, and I was glad that despite the city's effort to tame the roadside, the ice had enough wild to work with. It made do.

These, however, I do not lick.

I did find one honey locust pod that didn't rattle when I shook it. It was rusty brown, nearly as long as my forearm, and sure enough, inside between seeds was still goopy and sweet. The taste is sort of like dates or fig, and with a smoky note best savored on a slow exhale, mouth shut. I was in a hurry now, and I sucked the torn end on the way to school, driving fast past drifts of frost flower—four feet tall—that I had not seen on the way in, along the shadowed side of the highway.

Liriodendron tulipifera

Listen to the music of a tulip poplar's name: *Leer-ee-oh-DEN-drun too-lip-PIFF-ur-uh*.

"It sounds like a spell from Harry Potter," my boy says. Surely there are wands made of it.

Izzy has been home sick for a week and will miss tomorrow's test on Tennessee symbols. At the kitchen table he drew the homework mockingbird and iris and passionflower and tulip poplar tree, and colored them with pencils from the old cigar box. He also drew Elvis.

None of these things is at school. The closest tulip poplar is across the street, but the kids don't know that.

In spring blooms of a tulip poplar look like orange-yellow-green tulips. Leaves are shaped like folk art tulip silhouettes. But the tree is neither tulip nor poplar; it is a magnolia.

I could bring his class my framed poster of Young Elvis, but I can't bring a bird, and my passion vine is December brown and my irises are dormant.

So today I left my son at home and brought a cardboard tray to his teacher who said "yes, please" to

a stack of soft tulip poplar leaves, still autumn yellow
   (one per kid)

a seed cluster on a twig (a clue to ID the tree in winter)

a curled leaf full of loose seeds (helicopters!)

an info sheet with pictures of tulip poplar leaf, seeds,
   twig, flower

On her desk at the whiteboard, I left a pickle jar filled with
orange hothouse tulips. Because you can't understand tulip
poplar if you can't understand tulip.

They for sure don't know what a poplar is, but that's okay.
She told me they all say "popular" anyway.

Hummingbird Winter

At 6:18 in the morning the hummingbird feeder looks more brown than red, but suddenly she's on it. She is the size of my thumb, she weighs less than a nickel, and all I see is a glowy white throat in daybreak gloom. My winter hummingbird. She should be in Mexico by now, or Central America, but she is here in my Nashville yard, with frozen seed heads of goldenrod. She looks around, bends her head, and then drinks for nine long minutes.

Nine minutes is long enough for the sky to fade through several paint chip colors, for a squirrel to creep from the soffit vent. Long enough for robins first heard but not seen, then seen leaving cedar roosts for the bare hackberry, and for the first crow to flap overhead and *caw*. Long enough for a siren on the interstate to come, to go. And now, the *plink plink* of hackberry fruit dropping—or is that robin droppings?

"Why do you love the hummingbird so much?" my son asked yesterday, and I did not know how to answer. How can I not love it? How can I not help her do whatever it is she needs to do?

Headlines tell me that in my lifetime North America has lost nearly three billion birds. My eyeballs tell me birds are losing habitat every day, even here in our city neighborhood, with every infill bulldozer, every lawncare pesticide, every yard that does not include the native plants that support our food web. Hummingbirds need more than sugar water and nectar; they need the tiny creatures who make a living on plants: caterpillars, spiders, gnats, aphids, and even mosquitoes. I watch my bird glean invisible someones from cedar needles, from fluffy tips of dried frostweed.

It was chance that in late October I saw the invitation to keep hummingbird feeders up through winter and chance that it worked: my bird appeared three weeks later. The next day Cyndi Routledge—a federally licensed master bird-bander—drove fifty miles to my driveway to catch, identify, and band what turned out to be a hatch-year ruby-throated hummingbird with zero fat and hardly a tail feather. She taught me that hummers are more resilient than they look, their migration behavior is more flexible than we thought, and they don't stay where they can't survive.

"How long will this one stay?" I asked Cyndi, hoping she'd say forever.

"It could leave tomorrow or stay indefinitely," she shrugged. "If it goes, it'll be with a north wind."

I shall stay until the wind changes, the bird said, but only in my head, and in the voice of Julie Andrews as Mary Poppins.

While Cyndi finished measuring and weighing and blowing and banding, I wondered how I could lick my finger in secret, to test the direction of the breeze. And then, with the bird still in hand, she stood up from my patio set, and I heard her asking me, as if it was no big deal: "You wanna hold it?"

Years ago, when my kids were little, we went to Warner Park for a hummingbird banding. After each bird was done, the naturalist—my friend Heather—would tell a waiting child, "Hold out your hand, and don't move," and then slowly, gently place a hummingbird in the child's flat palm. At that point birds are so stunned that they simply lie where they're put. Then Heather would ask, "Can you feel the heartbeat?

She put a bird in my daughter's hand. She put one in my son's hand.

"Can you feel the heartbeat?"

"Yes," they whispered. "Yes."

Not until my driveway moment did I realize that more than anything else, I wanted to feel the heartbeat of a hummingbird. Not until Cyndi said, "You wanna hold it?"

Yes.

Nine minutes is long enough for a breeze to turn the feeder and show the hummingbird's profile. I can see how she's fluffed her body against the cold. If the sky were lighter, I'd see the wink of metal that links her to me. But this breeze feels new. It makes me check the weather app on my phone where, sure enough, there's the letter I've been dreading. The wind is from the north.

I can tell you now: a hummingbird's heart doesn't beat. A beat is something you could count or tap, or at least discern from one unit to the next. But my hand didn't beat; it vibrated.

A hummingbird heart hums.

Because of the Dashboard

The bag sailed over five lanes of traffic near Green Hills mall. I thought it was a bird, because I always check the sky at red lights, and this thing was high and slow and soaring.

The breeze had puffed the plastic bag big and round. It was a mouth, eating air at leisure, tumbling, gliding, revolving as it floated west. My mouth was open too, the better to hinge my neck to follow the bag against the widest possible field of morning blue: through the windshield, the driver's window; over the nail salon, the fancy jewelers, the cigar shop. In a few seconds it would be over Trader Joe's, and if the breeze held it might drift straight back home, to Kroger.

This was a Kroger bag all right, although too high to let me read the logo. Our big grocery chain insists on offering plastic bags the color of paper bags—the standard kraft color. Why is it that brown paper bags are pretty but brown plastic bags are not? Kraft bags are iconic. They are a pleasure to touch, fold, tear, cut, and draw upon with pencil, pen, marker, crayon, charcoal, and paint, and especially with tempera paint fresh from a wetting in a non-spill kindergarten cup. And yet the same color transposed to a plastic bag, which has the same function at the same store, is ugly.

Looking around my kitchen right now, I see more kraft color: a cotton napkin I dyed with walnuts. A dry sycamore leaf. A half-whittled stick. A yellowwood pod. Ironweed fluff. A jar of pecans. A dead spitting spider. Demerara sugar. All of these things are the light brown of a Kroger bag, all are lovely. But the crinkled bag I am using for reference is not lovely, either aesthetically or ethically. It is an ecological villain: a choking, clogging, petroleum-based, nonbiodegradable, past-and-future pelletized plastic menace.

Of course, we aren't supposed to be using any of these bags, paper or plastic, pretty or not. We are supposed to remember the hand-me-down reusable totes stacked in the hatchback of my car. And I do for the most part, but when we forget, bags accumulate. I fold and keep the paper ones. But I layer the plastic ones inside each other one by one. Eventually they swell into a grotesque sphere of a matryoshka doll too enormous to fit through the lid of the recycle bin designated for them at Kroger.

So it was an ugly Kroger bag is what I'm saying. The bag I watched fly over Green Hills.

By the way, the greenest thing about Green Hills is the green, green money spent here. Traffic to the mall is snarly all day, every day, and I avoid it, but I do have to pass through to get to Whole Foods, where my own green goes once a week. And when I watched the Kroger bag fly, I wasn't at a red light but had been detained beside what will be the tallest, widest footprint of a mixed-use high-rise built in Green Hills and which will generate so very much more green. It's been rising for years. One of the construction guys walked into my lane to hold up his hand at me and the other Green Hills customers running errands during school hours. Both lanes dutifully braked, not sorry for the opportunity to peek again at our phones.

Meanwhile a dump truck made a tortured five-point turn in order to cut ahead of us. I looked up, and there was the bag. And it wasn't ugly: it was exquisite. I was lost in this bag. I wanted to be this bag. At the very least, I wanted to watch while it flew, while it rode that updraft, while it lazed as slow as a lone turkey vulture, while it meandered so voluptuous; and while I was stuck in my car on a packed road, letting a truck cut line so it could get back all the quicker to finish these shops so more people can spend more green and make more traffic and need more bags.

The next morning I walked out of my medical gym thinking not of bags but of gloves. It was fifteen degrees. People say polar ice is why we get these crazy low temps, because we're melting the ice crazy fast thanks to our crazy need for things like disposable bags. My gloves had been my grandmother's, and like everything she owned, they were pristine. I'd recently filched them from my mom's hoard of winter surplus. They still smelled like an old pressed powder compact, the kind with a monogram and a mirror and a slippery pad. Come to think of it, the gloves were the same color as her powder would have been, what used to be called nude back when people who thought up color names didn't consider that not all skin colors are "nude" when nude.

Anyway, outside the gym I got to the river birch at the corner and looked down. At my ankles was another Kroger bag. Empty like the flying one, but filthy inside and out with I don't know what kind of gray mess. It was trash, and I pick up trash. But I hesitated. Would I ruin my dead grandmother's gloves? Would her stretchy 1980s vinyl still smell of racist face powder? I bent down, but as soon as I did the bag skidded through the intersection toward the children's hospital. So I chased it and risked it and pinched it as lightly as I could, and I carried it to my car floorboard where it felt right at home with all the other trash I generate or find. And I thought, Wouldn't it be funny if this was the glorious bag of yesterday? The bag I wanted to be? Depending on the breeze, it could well have been. I was on the same road. Although as plastic bags are the number one consumer item on the planet and a pollutant so ubiquitous that many cities have passed ordinances against them, the odds are not in favor of such a romantic notion. And even if it was the same bag, it sure wasn't pretty now.

Why am I telling you about a pretty bag and an ugly bag? I am not altogether sure, but it is something to do with complicating nature, with thinking of nature in a more complicated way. I keep hearing that nature has to be scenery, or park, or badass wilderness, or extreme outdoor challenge, or, at the very least, forest or flower. But nature is also a flying Kroger bag in Nashville traffic.

Some people go to nature to escape. But no one can escape nature. We are already there.

One of my favorite books of nature writing is Annie Dillard's *Pilgrim at Tinker Creek*. "I explore the neighborhood," Dillard tells us near the start, yet nowhere in her masterful, magical, singular, solo exploration of that neighborhood does she tell us it was a suburb. Tinker Creek was in view of houses, people, driveways, cars.

Last night Michael was driving us home from a friend's house on the river. I was starstruck with the idea of the Cumberland River as backyard and wasn't paying attention to the road. Then Michael oohed at the setting sun and asked me to take a picture for him, and Izzy and I looked up and saw the rim of an orange blob above the horizon, which right then was an overpass on Interstate 40. The sun was massive.

"It's changing every millisecond," Michael yelled, negotiating lanes at the junction with Interstate 24, whose loops opened a comprehensive view of backlit clouds. The three of us drank every drop of orange until it was gone and then as good as licked the sky.

When I got home I looked at my dozen or so photos and realized I had framed each one to include the car dashboard. Quite a bit of dashboard. If I had aimed higher, I could have easily missed our car, even missed most of the interstate. And even now I could crop out a few semi-trailers. But here's the thing: the orange blob and the entire color-washed sky, with pink and blue and lavender clouds and with watercolor wispies and gray clots and fanned textures that looked like cellulite but in a good way—my instincts told me the view was all the more beautiful because of the dashboard. And because of the trucks and the on-ramps. And because of the white headlights and red taillights coming and going from the same vanishing point as the sun's own point of vanishing. These things frame the sky in my pictures because they frame it in real life when we drive home on I-40 at the right time. Because this tension between nature and stuff people make is nature too. Flying bags and all.

Winter Solstice

I needed a bonfire to welcome the sun. All the wood and kindling are soaked from days of rain, but I did warm two pine cones to smoking point. It'll have to do. I was happy to inhale even this bit of pagan spark and heat at high noon (or low noon, given the date). Smoke snaked over Next Door's privacy fence as if it could not get away fast enough.

That's when peripheral vision told me I wasn't alone. The ground was bubbling. It was erupting. Sugar maple leaves were hoisting themselves from our yard in somersaults: dozens of them, here, there. Every flip whispered *pshhh, pshh* in surround sound. When I focused on one *pshh* at a time, I saw the robins, at least forty of them, and the nearest only a few feet away. Each one was shoveling leaves with their head. Scoop, pause, scoop, pause, scoop. Not that I was surprised to see robins in late December or even so many at once. Some robins migrate to Nashville, some migrate from Nashville, some stay, and whoever happens to be here hangs out together.

What surprised me was how I didn't notice I was mid-flock as I walked from the house with my matchbox and as I struggled with my pine cones. Today, winter solstice, when most leaves are down, robins are camouflaged in space and time. They match the yard. Those wide breasts *are* sugar maple leaves: the male's rust is the upper leaf surface, the female's peach is the underneath. Gray-brown wings and heads are old elm leaves, hackberry leaves, and the mud where our dog's feet uproot even the crabgrass. Oblique sun mosaics all these colors in glare and glow and shadow. Winter light is crooked. Winter light is the sun with a migraine.

The robins do not mind me.

What are they searching for? Robins don't want my black oil sunflower by the birdbath; they eat invertebrates and fruit. Most insects are dead or underground by now. Winter ants should be active, but I haven't checked. There may be the odd grass spider or thawed woolly worm, and last week I did hear a field cricket at dusk.

The obvious plenty is fruit: hackberry drupes are *everywhere*, having been blown or nudged from the five mature trees that hug the yard. But if the robins fancy a hackberry all-you-can-eat buffet they have only to walk or hop—because unlike some birds they can do both—a few feet to the driveway, where hundreds of sweet garnet-colored BBs roll free, and with no masking mat of leaves. No need for shovels.

Maybe sometimes even robins don't see what is in front of them. Not when the sun has a migraine.

The birds would have to share driveway hackberries with our dog and with me. A hackberry is sweet but subtle. Think fruit leather, buttery, deep, though the flesh is no thicker than construction paper. Several foragers say they taste like dates. They do, but you have to work for it. Pop a fat smooth hackberry "berry" in your mouth, and roll it between teeth and tongue to suck pumpkin-colored meat from bony pit. Spit the pit wherever a baby hackberry can sprout in spring to host butterfly eggs laid in leaf axils. Or spit the pit into your hand to admire wrinkles on a brain the size of a peppercorn. If your teeth are up to it, crack the brain and taste the soft kernel inside: green but paler than the two seed leaves it was hoping to sprout later. I don't recommend pliers, because they crush the whole thing flat.

Our dog doesn't go to this trouble. Beatrice swallows drupes without chewing, which is what robins do. Last year Michael took a photo of me in the driveway with Bea, where she and I both gobbled hackberries from the asphalt. I was squatting in my thickest parka plucking drupes one at a time with ungloved pincer grip. And because it is rare to be eating the same thing at the same time and off the same ground with one's dog, every so often I would center one hackberry in my bare palm and offer it to her. She'd stop foraging and turn to me and kiss her whiskered chin to my skin and make the hackberry disappear.

What am I searching for today? Why do I want a bonfire at lunchtime? Why do I imagine a personal, suburban tribute to the sun necessary? And how can the charring of two pine cones offer a satisfactory nod to the tilt of the northern hemisphere?

I've read that technically, astronomically, the solstice lasts three days. Time stands still, sort of, before moving in the sun's favor. So technically, astronomically, I have two more days to dry wood and make a real fire. Or to at least find the box of sparklers left over from the Fourth of July.

A memory is surfacing. Years ago, when my parents still lived at the house where I grew up, when my sister's three kids were little and my one child even littler, I helped everyone gather noisemakers where we could find them: anything that could be a drum or rattle, which was a lot, considering the marvels of junk at hand. This is when the word "solstice" entered family vocabulary. We waded through two garages to the backyard—on the far side of the wildflower island I had planted for Dad to see from his recliner by the window—and marched in a circle, banging and rattling and yelling our welcome to the sun. Was there a fire? There must have been. Dad marched too, and in my head he is in flannel pajamas. And after we were back inside and scattered, my sister stood in the kitchen and said, "You know this is because of you, right? This kind of thing doesn't happen without you."

Was it winter solstice or summer? Were we telling the sun hello or goodbye? Either way, I made a thing happen. I usually react to waves, not make waves for others to react to. I am grateful my sister made me notice then and now.

This gives me one answer to today's what and why. I need some kind of marker—any time, all the time, but especially at a major calendrical shift—because without one, minutes and hours and days and years and decades slide into one another without a guide, without an accounting.

This year my sister and mom and my sister's oldest spent the solstice watching the sun sink into the Pacific Ocean, watching the moon rise right after, and building a bona fide bonfire by the shore. "With marshmallows," Mom added. I am happy for them. But I am happy to be here at home. For me, two pine cones will do. As will standing in crooked light among forty busy robins who pay me no mind.

Raptor Ready

At the red light halfway to Hebrew School I usually check my phone or glance at my kid in his booster or blink at the soccer field, but the day is winter warm and the open window pulls my eye to a Methodist church: midcentury concrete block straight up, up to a cross like a giant rust lollipop with arms.

"Red-tailed hawk on the steeple," I yell. "See it?"

I see it so fast it feels *beshert*, meant to be: *Buteo jamaicensis*, female, huge, on the lollipop's right hand. Blurred brown, white on the belly, mantle feathers askew.

Redtails are not rare—they nest in trash trees on the limestone cliffs of the I-440 bypass. But wherever or whenever I see a hawk, normal life stops.

I may as well be a character in a fairy story. I may as well be in a wonder tale. I may as well fly out of my Toyota miniwagon right now to join her, and I may as well bring my boy too. We slide through our windows and rise. We catch a thermal and float. We toss our glasses because we are hawkeyed. We thirst for dove and squirrel. Our tennis shoes, like her talons, grip the chicken wire on the lollipop's transverse beam, wire put there by church committee to repel birds.

She is not a bird. She is a god.

I hope the red light lasts an eternity.

She scours empty air over the soccer kids, over us, over rich people houses beyond, over the slow road we wait to join.

"That's funny—a hawk on a cross. Like Jesus, right?" says my small Jewish child, who knows no better.

Accidental Glade

It's the day before Christmas Eve, and someone has dumped birdseed on the parking lot at Hamilton Creek Recreation Area. This is at the lonelier side of the lonely dead end at a lonely cove: the farthest from the mountain bike trail, past the little playground, beyond the summer kiosk. An act of kindness here is a surprise. I am not surprised someone has spray-painted the asphalt with a giant white penis mid-squirt onto a pair of boobs, but I am betting it is not the same someone.

When we walk the accidentally conserved glade land here—even during summer when the lake might have paddleboarders and the swing set might have toddlers—I feel like we're in a Stephen King novel. Either I am about to find a dead body or become one.

Michael uses "urban pastoral" to describe this place the Army Corps of Engineers carved from weedy rock near the dam. I use "creepy." Fresh trash is a constant: beer cans, red Solo cups, shotgun shells, tobacco wrappers, clothing. More Gatorade empties than anyone should see in a lifetime roll through the locked BMX compound beyond the birdseed. But here's the thing: we see the trash but never the trashers.

It's like post–zombie apocalypse land or, given the demographics, post-Rapture, and this Jewish family has rightly been Left Behind. The whole property feels menacing. To me, anyway. Michael says he's "walked alone here fifty times over the years" to hunt fossils and wander through the woods, but then again he is a self-described blithe spirit. I am a suspicious spirit.

As if on cue, as soon as we emerge from the car today (by the penis, as it happens), another car appears but far too slowly, and it cruises, cruises toward our otherwise deserted and obvious dead end. I do not know whether to scoot back inside and scream at Michael to start the engine, ready my phone for a 911, or stroll toward the woods as if I too am blithe. The driver avoids eye contact, drawls a U-turn, and cruises, cruises away.

The security cameras haven't worked for years. The city doesn't have the budget to update the software. And, thanks to a news story after a nanny in charge of kids was attacked here last fall, everyone knows that the security cameras haven't worked for years.

Here's where I notice the birds. Chickadees and tufted titmice peck at a spattering on the asphalt, which of course I assume is last night's vomit. I inspect it anyway because how can I not, and wouldn't the image make a good haiku? But I'm wrong. It is not barf. It is a gift. It is Premium Wild Mix: black oil sunflower, millet, peanut, safflower, and cracked corn. Three piles are spaced as separate snack bars. They are at the transition of pavement to soil, and near a line of low bushy cedars for cover. Care was taken.

The birds evaporate at our coming.

We start our walk at the BMX track. Know that there are people to whom you must explain what BMX means, and people to whom you do not. (Bicycle motocross.) We skirt the humped lanes and shuttered snack shack to veer toward the lake. But today's goal isn't to walk along shore rocks, but to walk on the weirder ones that wrinkle and rise from the thin woods: limestone pavements.

Imagine a series of flat-topped, roughly rectangular chunks of limestone—horizontal bedding planes—elevated above soil by a foot or two or more, fantastically pitted by erosion, stippled with fossils, sometimes sculpted into arches or bridges or toadstools, and often gouged in what look like claw marks or big bites of a backhoe. All the work of water. Imagine leaping from boulder to boulder and not touching the ground. Not that I manage more than cautious hops. I worry about rattlesnakes basking on the mossy plateaus, I worry about falling when smaller rocks pivot, I worry about leaping onto what I think is mud under leaf litter but what is actually a limestone fissure the right size to eat my boot and break my ankle. I worry.

Cedars and young hickories have taken root where they can, as has trash. Fishing lines and lures tell me a lot of the latter has been pushed by lake and trapped by rock. Privet and bush honeysuckle are trash too, brought by berry and bird, and if this weren't winter I'd worry about what was on the still green, whippy branches that smack me as we muscle through, but it is too cold for ticks today. In spring, summer, or fall I'd be flicking dozens off my body by now.

Privet flushes us toward the access road, up to glade land.
I call it accidental because it feels accidental. Why would
anyone save moss and lichen and rocks and thin soil on
purpose? We figure because Metro Parks runs recreation
hubs near a dam, the land between trailheads and marinas
and racetracks and parking lots can stay land. It can't be
bulldozed and parceled and served up as another lakeside
condo community with a nature name that ends in Pointe
with an e: Heron Pointe, Woodland Pointe. Some of this
land is glade. And somehow Michael found it.

Bright green moss snugs both shoulders of the access
road. It claims nearly every chunk of roadside gravel trucked
here to bed the asphalt, and I think of it as beating what cut
it, like "paper covers rock" in a game of rock-paper-scissors.
A few steps up, the moss morphs into shag carpet with gold
highlights: the true glade moss (*Pleurochaete squarrosa*).
And here are puddles of bare limestone white in the sun but
never truly bare. Even the black pepper specks are a lichen,
probably older than we are. Next to charred bones of illegal
campfires are nostoc curls green and rubbery, white snail
shells, moss shaped like stars, a winter ant on cedar needles
the same rust color as herself, and reindeer lichen, an impossibly intricate network of crunchy twiglets. Prickly pear
cactus meets more moss up the hill, and I see a trail so subtle it must be made by deer for deer.

One tall ailanthus tree (there is never just one) clutches
fistfuls of seed and is now my landmark, because beside it
is a young hackberry I will visit again. You need to know
that Middle Tennessee is the hackberry capital of the world,

and that I love these warty everywhere trees, and that most everyone else hates them. People say hackberries are trash trees, which is true if by trash you mean they volunteer along fence lines. People say they are messy trees, which is true if by mess you mean food for wildlife. And people say they fall down in storms, which is true of any tree, but here's the thing: it seems as if more hackberries fall down than do any other tree, because Nashville has more hackberries than any other tree. And by the way, the bark is gorgeous and the fruit delicious, and the form of an open-grown hackberry can arch and umbrella and bouquet itself as gracefully as any American elm.

Anyway, this hackberry at the ailanthus marker is strangely cramped, and almost every one of its zigzag buds—usually spear tips pressed against the twig—is puffed and smooth and round, almost the size and shape of the fruit that should be hanging off the twigs this time of year. Oh my goodness, they must be galls—bud galls— and I have never seen hackberry bud galls, and I hop with idiot glee on the roadside until I notice that I'm dislodging moss. I've seen hackberry leaf galls for ages, hackberry pet- iole galls for years, but never bud galls. Each type encases a different species of psyllid.

Know there is no one to whom you do not have to explain what psyllids are. Hackberry psyllids are teensy insects that harm nothing, feed warblers, are cute, and rely exclusively on hackberry trees from gall to grave.

I break the tip of a twig to pinch one bud. Two thumb- nails in tandem split it, and then I am washed in guilt to see orange-red specks of early instar larvae whose winter home I have destroyed. Sorry, guys.

I lay the gall on the ground. Maybe something hungry (and very small) can eat it? I want to go home and find out what the adults look like, what the life cycle is. Michael says maybe I've discovered a new species and I say without thinking that I'll name it after the park, but he interrupts with "No, Brichetto" and on the drive home I dream of immortality. A psyllid with my surname. What could be better?

At home I will learn that entomology has known about hackberry bud galls since before I was born. I will also learn that Hamilton Creek Recreation Area is an official bird-watching hot spot. Not only the bit of lake next to the graffiti and birdseed but the two nearby marinas. All three are lumped as one location, despite needing a car to get from one to the others. According to the latest eBird stats, as recently as two days ago someone reported a bufflehead, northern shoveler, gadwall, red-breasted merganser. All are waterbirds, which are what make this spot hot.

It still doesn't explain backyard birdseed in the parking lot.

Who brought it? A neighbor? A resident from Heron Pointe trying to mitigate the irony that her own home displaced habitat for herons? An eBirder who hopes to log a rare songbird? Was it tipped from a sack as a car cruised even slower than the car we'd seen? How often is seed replenished? And at the time, is the giver suspicious or blithe?

We scare every birdseed bird up to the cedars when we

step back in from BMX land. A titmouse fusses, though I cannot see it. I squat to take pictures of the miraculous seed. We both snap a pic of the penis and boobs, because this too, would make a good haiku. As we drive off, the birds come back: cardinal, blue jay, chickadee, mourning dove. But I don't look for long. In the car I am staring at urban pastoral photos of Premium Wild Mix in the foreground, asphalt in the middle, and, in the distance, one steely patch of man-made lake.

Discontinued

My grandfather sipped it standing up, his back to the kitchen sink, to the salt and pepper shakers shaped like hugging bears (Regal China, 1950s, discontinued), to the T-bar clothesline out the window, and to the cedar woods at the edge of his ever-mown lawn.

This was forty years ago in Lake City (discontinued 2014), formerly known as Coal Creek (discontinued 1936), and currently doing business as Rocky Top, Tennessee.

Who told my grandfather to drink hot water after meals? *Reader's Digest*? The pastor's wife? A doctor? "Horse doctor," my mom would spit, whenever she heard what a local quack said or did to her parents.

He had poured water from the hot tap, cloudy, into one of the bumpy green glass tumblers (Anchor Hocking, Soreno Avocado, discontinued). Not the orange mugs with grandkids' names written in ballpoint on masking tape (Fire King, D handle stackable milk glass, discontinued). I know because I could see the pale swill inside and wonder why anyone would punish themselves with hot sink water. It was a shame to wash down Grandmother's green beans, mashed potatoes, and dredged-in-cornmeal, fried-in-cast-iron crappie with not even sweet tea, not even hot tea or Mr. Coffee coffee.

He didn't seem to mind. His eyes and his voice—when he had something to say—stayed soft. He did have hard skills. Paw could build anything, and did: vegetable gardens, a tractor, his house, Norris dam. Even with black lung, he brought home deer, squirrel, Cove Lake fish. He gave us fish bladders to toss like little balloons.

The horse doctor never noticed that my grandfather had intestinal polyps, so many and so big they were seeable from the outside. That's what killed him: colon cancer, not coal mines.

Last month a macrobiotic guru here in Nashville told me to drink hot water after meals. I'm healing a hole in my stomach, put there by pills from doctors. At least I hope that's what this pain is.

"Spring water," she prescribed, "heated over gas flame. And no more tea."

There is no potable spring in town. Tap water has chlorine and fluoride. Hot tap would be worse; warmth pulls lead all the quicker from galvanized pipe and old solder. And my house, alas, is not laid for gas. I compromise with jugs of reverse-osmosis Whole Foods water decanted into a crock, and with an electric kettle, even though "electricity is not a healing energy."

I sip it standing up, my back to the kitchen sink, to the sea salt and flaxseed shakers, to the pulley clothesline out the window, and to the cedar at the edge of my never mown lawn.

I use the mug from England (Churchill Blue Willow, Georgian shape, discontinued) and pretend I am holding— as I have held nearly every day since college—PG Tips tea from a five-minute steep in a warmed china pot.

But it is only hot water.

I don't know where the bear salt and pepper shakers went, or the green tumblers, or the Fire King mugs, but I could get them all online easily. Replacements Ltd. has a huge database of patterns, and there's always eBay. I already have Grandmother's old everyday china (Paden City Ivy, gold on edge, discontinued). She told me years ago, before she moved to assisted living, that I could have it if that's what I wanted, if it meant something to me, and that she and Paw had bought it in Clinton when they first "set up housekeeping." It's in a box in my basement, wrapped in yellowed grocery fliers from her ShopRite (108 Creek Street, discontinued). Maybe I will switch to one of those cups and saucers just for the now, just while I miss my tea and my stomach lining.

Maybe they will make the hot water taste better.

And do me more good than it did him.

Opportunity

On Christmas Day, as my Jewish family drove to our "faith tradition"—a Chinese buffet—we saw something wild. Dozens and dozens of white gulls were spiraling over the old Kmart lot at the corner of Harding Place and Nolensville Road. A quick U-turn brought us directly underneath, along with four other cars that had stopped to stare.

The lot is about five miles (as the gull flies) from the nearest water—Radnor Lake, the Cumberland River, Percy Priest Lake—which doesn't sound far, but it feels far. The Kmart lot feels like it's a hundred miles from anything wetter than a storm sewer. It anchors a vast, empty corner of these two main roads and would, I imagine, be easy to spot from the air. It might even look a bit like a dead gray lake.

It was alive now. The gulls flew, landed, flew, restless, on their own or in tiered waves. We could see gray atop the wings—the color called dove gray as if doves get all the credit—and a splash of black ink at wing tips. When gulls stood, black fingers extended past the tail. When they flew, black reached wide. And when they flew, they spoke in the squeals and squawks of beach language, of ocean. The one puddle on the asphalt was a target, and they took turns aiming touchdowns at it. It was too shallow to drink, but the patch of silver, from where we were sitting, mirrored gull underbellies and dull sky.

We don't see gulls every day, and certainly not in such numbers, and we were fascinated—in the original sense of the word—magicked, bewitched. We could not look away.

There is a lot of lot here. Too much. Whoever planned this long-gone Kmart could not have foreseen Walmart, Target, Costco, or worse, Amazon Prime. And a lonely spot like this—overlarge and underused but situated at the intersection of two six-lane arteries—acquires a flavor. The flavor is failure. With a whiff of sinister, especially after you note the volume of trash at the privet-choked edge, because broken furniture is never a good omen when it shows signs of frequent use by persons not currently in view. If I wrote a place-based horror novel I'd cast this whole corner as a Nashville hellmouth. And in the story, as would happen in real life, when word got out that the property was a hellmouth half of Nashville would say, "Oh, of course, the Kmart lot. I knew there was something weird about that place."

Poor Kmart. Taking Martha Stewart on board was a coup, until she went to jail. Before that and after, the celebrity spokesperson was a star from the 1970s, which is the decade Kmart never left. Although in the 1980s my Knoxville store was the first to offer a fancy new kind of bag at checkout. This was the predecessor of the bags everyone uses now, except in cities where they've been outlawed as the environmental disasters they've become. If there is a hellmouth attribute or emblem, it is a plastic sack. As Saint Catherine has her wheel and Saint Sebastian his arrows, so the hellmouth has petroleum-based bags.

But at the moment, the hellmouth had birds.

Another car cruised in to stare. The birds moved, but the watchers didn't. I only looked away from the gulls long enough to check out the other people checking out the gulls. And to notice what they drove and what they wore, and to guess that none of us had much in common except for a momentary fascination with a tornado of seabirds in a parking lot on Christmas Day.

The man behind the wheel of a white lowrider yelled, "Heyyyyyy, hey, HEY!" to lure the gulls, somehow, closer to his camera. The women on the far side of the lot were standing beside their cars taking videos. We all looked happy. Giddy, even: struck with wonder.

When I got home I learned that the Kmart gulls are regulars. They've showed up in winter flocks longer than Kmart itself stayed in business. Some locals know this and bring food on purpose: cheap birdseed, bags of bread, a box of Cheerios. But the sure thing is a stream of chance passersby who fling edibles out their car windows. It's Nolensville Pike—the heart of Nashville's ethnic eateries—so there is no shortage of fabulous food in those cars. Although a Hardee's drive-through shares the parking lot, so offerings are probably heavy on the fries.

I found the evidence online with search terms "Nolensville Road" and "seagull." I did this knowing that proper birders do not use the term "seagull." I wanted social media posted by improper birders. Civilians. Their cumulative evidence judged the Kmart "seagulls" were "crazy!" "lost!" "confused!" and "a long way from the ocean!" Although the latter is true it doesn't matter, and the other adjectives aren't true at all. Gulls are not that gullible. They know a good meal when they see it.

Our Kmart gulls had black rings around their bills, and I was pleased to discover they've been given the sensible name ring-billed gulls. Audubon tells me they are the gulls most likely to tornado in a Nashville parking lot far from water and on Christmas Day. They are opportunistic feeders. They are the panhandling pigeons of the marine bird world. Look for them too in landfills and dumps. Nashville is on the migration route, but some stay. And many, so I hear from local (proper) birders, were born on the Great Lakes and have never seen the sea. The gulls weren't lost and crazy: they were home and they were hungry.

As were we. We tore ourselves from the gulls to fly to another lot on the same road but packed with cars, even though the only thing open was the Chinese buffet. On another day you could buy quinceañera dresses, rent furniture, get a haircut, shop for phones, eat shawarma. There is a Latino nightclub, an "Indo-Pak-Bangla" grocery, and two markets that call themselves international. It's a scruffy old strip mall but with no whiff of sinister, no taste of failure. This is one of those places where the American dream renews itself continually, shop by shop. It's like a real version of the urban myth where the human body replaces itself, cell by cell, every few years.

The flock at the buffet was diverse, unlike the gulls, and all the more so after we arrived as the sole representatives of Jewish People. Our server wished us a Merry Christmas at least five times and nearly levitated with joy, and we couldn't help but be happy right back at her. And let me say how much this Jewish family loves Christmas Day. Not the season, but the day. Because every day for the previous three weeks we have been wished by strangers and cashiers and acquaintances and neighbors to have a Merry Christmas, which is fine and sweet but also clueless and presumptuous and how exactly are we supposed to respond? It's not like Jews walk around Nashville on Friday afternoons wishing everyone Shabbat Shalom. We don't wish all and sundry a happy Hanukkah or Rosh Hashanah or Yom Kippur or Sukkot or Tu BiShvat or Purim or Passover, because we don't assume everyone within greet range celebrates the same holidays we do. Are we to teach people that not every single human celebrates Christmas? To do so would take tact and time and I doubt we have enough of either, so we parrot the greeting back to the greeter, sincerely but also with a quick mental calculation of how many more days until the actual, real, greeting-worthy day of Christmas.

In graduate school, one of Michael's best friends asked him what Jews do on Christmas. She felt sorry for him. "Do you just sit around and mope?"

Nope. We sit around and eat Chinese. Because that's what's open.

There was more than Chinese food at this buffet. There were tables and tables of sushi, salads, sweets, soups, a cook-to-order grill, casseroles, plantain, kabobs, a whole table of shellfish we ignore, a whole table of deep-fried crap we do not ignore, and tons of "American"—pizza, roast beef, catfish, mac and cheese, fried chicken, and so forth. "All you can eat." The price was the only moderate thing in sight.

Speaking of American, do the young women who take drink orders get vexed when customers answer not with "sweet tea" or "Diet Coke" but with "Where are you from?" The staff is Asian American, but the diners are everything but, and very few of us are white. So, fellow white diners who have not thought about this before, let me tell you that "Where are you from?" might not be the friendliest greeting. It means "Where is your real home, because you are not home here."

We flocked, we fed. Hundreds of us, united in fascination with an obscene amount of food. We slalomed with plates in hand, veered around steam trays, leaned in for samples, scooped this and that, tweezed the best gobbets, dug for the drumstick, slapped our kids away from the ice cream. We weren't a tornado; we were more like a prevailing wind. But the buffet was a people-food landfill, a food fantasia, an extravagant dump. And like the Kmart lot, it was heavy on the fries.

I obsessed about the gulls for days. Weeks. I made notes. I drew a concept map. I researched Kmart.

When I was little, Kmart's blue-light special was a wonder. It was an actual blue light, wheeled to whichever product had been selected for a limited time price cut. The where and when was announced on the intercom, and shoppers would literally run to the light. Some abandoned their carts to run faster, flock like gulls. One time I looked up to see the blue light wheeling toward me in the school supplies aisle, and I skedaddled because no school supplies—no matter how fragrant the cedar pencils—are worth that much tzimmes. "Tzimmes" is a Yiddish word I was decades away from learning, but it means a "big fuss," and I still prefer to watch big fusses from a safe distance.

I finally asked Michael to help me understand my struggle with the gulls. I told him about species and behavior, and he speculated that maybe the birds were the "pinnacle of evolution," because they thrive despite the mess we make of the world. He's right. Pest species are winners. Songbirds (and nearly everyone else) are losers. We make trash. Gulls eat trash. They are opportunists. The collective noun for a flock is a "scavenging" of gulls. Also, a squabble, a screech, and a flotilla. But I vote for a new collective noun for the ring-billed gulls who adapt so well to our dystopia. How about an "opportunity" of gulls?

I still couldn't figure out what was eating me about these birds. It couldn't be my fear of blue-light specials, could it? Or about how puberty and Kmart embarrassment bloomed at the same time, and the only thing worse than being seen in a Kmart—which at least meant seer and seen were both present and therefore humiliated—was being seen in a middle school with a Kmart tag still dangling from a waistband?

As a jobless adult in search of cheap, I shopped at the seagull Kmart. One time I took little Maggie to the boys department for basketball shorts and jerseys, and when we stood in line to pay the man behind us, who insisted on making conversation, asked Maggie if she was on a team. She tried to smile back and either she or I or both of us said yes, though she was not, in fact, part of any organized sport. She just wanted to look sporty. Those double-knit shorts pilled and picked something awful. It was the type of loose weave that grabs every rough surface, and when I tossed them in the trash a week later I thought, Oh, of course, Kmart.

A few days ago Michael and I were on an evening dog walk. A mockingbird kvetched at us from the top of his usual stop sign. This same bird guards this bit of sidewalk year-round and dive-bombs whomever comes near: other birds, squirrels, dogs, and sometimes us. Mockingbirds sing pretty, but they mean business. We stood staring at him staring at us, and that's when Michael asked, "By the way, did you get a good look at a gull? Up close?"

And I knew exactly what he meant.

From a distance, as a group, a collective, an "opportunity," the gulls are magic. They shock us with beauty even while they swarm in hopes of a handout in the hellmouth. Their air show compels busy people to veer into a parking lot we all know will be impossible to exit by a left turn later. We gather as strangers to gawk and marvel, to try and interact and be part of the tzimmes, because we can't fly. How often are civilians so moved by birds they have to show it off on social media? #wild!

An opportunity of gulls is a slice of heaven in the hellmouth. It's a blue-light special.

But only if you don't look too closely. Because one gull alone is bigger than you thought. The one bird, for example, who stands a few feet from your car window you are suddenly glad can shut at the press of a button. The bird is looking at you, and it is looking big. That pale eye with the black dot is reptilian, ancient. It is the eye of a velociraptor. You imagine this eye would make a good graphic logo on T-shirts (and plastic sacks) should the hellmouth be in need of branded swag. You have read about gulls and know there are some who blind baby seals in order to eat them—alive—at leisure. And you are struck by a cold certainty that this yellow beak with the pretty black band that looks like a smudge of makeup pencil, or like one of your black ponytail elastics, or a wash of India ink from a no. 8 round brush— this same beak would as soon pluck your eyeball from the socket as it would a French fry from a Hardee's bag.

Because like most things, it's all a matter of opportunity.

Sidewalk Fig

Pick me, begs the fig hanging over the street.

Every morning, I resist the temptation to pluck a fig from a sidewalk tree. I walk before dawn, but the plump silhouette is clear against the brightening sky.

Pick me.

I've watched this fig grow from the size of a chocolate chip to the size of a... fig. There are dozens on offer: stem-down, bottoms-up candy for strangers. But I keep walking. Someone might be looking out a window.

The tree stands in a hellstrip between street and sidewalk, but it's the nearest street-side fig that calls. It hangs at shoulder height, and as I pass I imagine how easy it would be to finger that fig from its place to my pocket.

The tree is probably a Brown Turkey, a cultivar that can cope with Nashville winters. It is self-fertile and sets fruit without the help of fig wasps—or any pollinator. But this fruit looks like it needs help to find eaters; our local squirrels, raccoons, possums, and birds have not yet noticed that figs are food.

On the one hand, the tree belongs to the neighbor who planted it. On the other hand, the tree is in a public right-of-way. On the other, other hand, what if everyone felt entitled to pluck a fig as they walked past? The twigs would be bare within hours.

But figs are figs: Mediterranean treasures not often found dangling above a Nashville street. Unless you happen to walk that street every single day.

Pick me! the fig said again this morning. It wore a dusting of frost. Then it added something new: words calculated to tempt me further, as it knows me so well.

I contain multitudes! it shouted, but it wasn't quoting Walt Whitman so much as describing itself: one fig is a composite fruit of many former flowers, a syconium. And as if I needed another fancy term to pique my interest, a fig is an example of parthenocarpy, the development of fruit without fertilization. Like virgin birth but for plants.

Figs are weird, wonderful, ancient. They're biblical, for god's sake. But except for one mealy pack from a grocery store, all my figs were in childhood Newtons. I have never in my life tasted a fresh fig, just plucked from a tree.

Yesterday I told my mom about the fig tree. We were walking back from the interstate bridge, where we had foraged about forty bruised and maggoty black walnut hulls from storm drains. Walnuts are delicious, but they take hours of messy labor to get from gross to good.

"Figs?" she asked. "You mean to tell me that there's ripe figs on the street, going begging?"

So this morning at dawn, when they beg, I take: a single fresh fig, just plucked from a tree.

Oh, Tannen-burn!

Once you start stealing Christmas trees, it's hard to stop. I've got three at the moment, but more will come. The best is the red cedar from the curb a block over. Izzy hauled it home, and I walked behind to watch it drag, long and tapered like a shut peacock tail.

January Christmas trees make great temporary brush piles for winter birds. They give cover to species loath to fly up to seed or suet high on poles. An example is the white-throated sparrow visiting from Canada. Asking one to spend all day on a tube feeder five feet off the ground is like asking me to spend happy hour on a barstool making chit-chat with strangers.

I pile trees near feeders by the kitchen window so we can watch two-level action. More animals show up and stay now that we offer cover. And in spring, when the needles are copper, Christmas trees burn like mad. You could let the chipper service collect them at the curb, or you could have a ton of fun watching bone-dry, resinous trees go up in flames.

I mention temporary brush piles because most people don't want great heaps of dead trees on their lawn. Especially if they use the word "lawn." Temporary is better than never.

We have yard, not lawn, so we keep at least one pile year-round. We add sticks Izzy and Beatrice bring home and prunings from the honeysuckles that refuse to die. In spring cottontails nest beneath and skinks bask on top. Chipmunks tunnel to escape cats or Cooper's hawks or us. In summer it gives the passion vine more acreage to sprawl. I dream of growing gourds on the rising pile, because this is one of those things I need to do at least once. Like canning pickles and boiling pokeweed and baking cake from the wild persimmons that fall in front of the AAA office. (Done, done, and done.) And like burning a bush for Hebrew School.

As an educator, my dream was to bring a dried Christmas tree to Hebrew School when first graders study the burning bush. To a kid, "burned, but was not consumed" has zero meaning. What better lesson for how fire usually consumes a bush than to watch fire eat one? And what better way than to let me drop a lit match on a desiccated cedar? *Sssssscrackle*, gone! This would be presented in contrast to the *Prince of Egypt* version, which not only keeps its leaves but keeps talking.

One time, when the Jewish holiday of trees (Tu BiShvat) fell in January, I did haul a Christmas tree to synagogue. A tree recycling dump is on my route to school, so it felt meant to be, *beshert*. I could steal a tight spruce, put a giant birthday hat on it, and ask the preschool to festoon it with objects that come from trees: toilet paper rolls, pine cones, fruit, wooden toys, paper chains, orange juice cartons, and so forth. We could sing Happy Birthday at it in Hebrew, on the official birthday of the trees. Adorable!

That Sunday morning I snuck to the tree-cycling drop-off at the park. It felt transgressive, so I snuck at dawn. This was a place for Christians to leave trees, not for Jews to take them. But oh, such waste, such riches! Not a mountain of trees but a mountain range: felled fir, spruce, pine, in all sizes. There were pitiful Charlie Brown trees, condo trees, we-have-twelve-foot-ceiling trees, we-hired-a-decorator trees, all sorts. Hundreds. There were the rule breakers Metro Parks warns against: trees covered in flocking, tinsel, lights, and trees wedged, nailed, and screwed to tree stands. They spilled three and four deep from the grass down onto the parking lot, where they hogged about a hundred feet of curb. That's when I noticed an identical forest heaped at the east entrance to the same park. And this was one tree-cycling site out of Nashville's twelve.

The smell of pitch hangs thick and powerful at these tree dumps. It's worth it to drive up and sit in the car with the window open. And though the fragrance comes from dead trees, it feels as if a few deep breaths could heal a body of anything.

That Sunday I sniffed and paced both sides of the mountains until I found my prize: a nice balsam fir. It was a couple of feet taller than I was and only slightly too heavy. Praying that no one would see, I rammed it into the car. I drove with the hatchback open to the empty synagogue lot and dragged the tree through the doors and down the hall into the art room. I wrangled it upright to wait in a corner while I cut and decorated a huge party hat from oversized posterboard. The hat was purple with polka dots and threaded with pastel ribbon through the tip. (No reds. No greens.) I climbed a chair to place this atop the birthday tree and then sat to admire the spectacle. Happy birthday, dear tree!

And then I had a panic attack.

I cannot bring a Christmas tree into a synagogue less than two weeks after Christmas. What was I thinking? It's a Christmas tree, no matter how loud we sing at it in Hebrew. And, oh my lord, I'd left a Hansel and Gretel trail of needles that led right to it, through the lot, the courtyard, and all along the carpets. No, no, no. I threw the hat into a closet and hauled that tree right back to the drop-off, praying that no one saw this Hebrew School teacher unloading what now looked like her family Christmas tree.

Fortunately I've gotten more relaxed about stealing trees. I raid anytime during January, not only at dawn. I even take extra trees to save for burning at leisure—equinoxes, solstices, special occasions. Once, when Maggie was home on winter break, we torched a tree in her honor. It was her first. She lit it and stepped back, and then farther back when the little tree showed that on a windless quiet dusk, it could blast flames four times its height.

I sent a photo of Maggie's tree to my sister Maria—a pyromaniac from infancy—and she said it brought back happy memories. She asked, "You know about Alex and his trees?" Alex is her youngest. She said that he and his buddy used to drive through the neighborhood after Christmas and nab trees where they found them. They'd line them up along Maria's endless chain-link fence, light the first one, and watch the whole row go. Like dominos but with fire.

I had not realized stealing Christmas trees ran in the family.

"Then one year," Maria went on, "they figured out that the lot where the Chick-fil-A is now was always a tree-selling spot. Christmas Day, the vendors would leave all the trees they didn't sell. Just sad clumps. Well, that's the year they gathered over a hundred." She said they burned an old piano too and, without permission, one of her Duncan Phyfe dining room chairs "because it was kinda broken."

My tree-cycling spot is at Elmington Park, which is not only on the way to Hebrew School but is on the way to any-thing west of us: Warner Park, Target, the Kroger that sells matzah, and our favorite Waffle House. It's the green space at the intersection of much of our lives, with Frisbee, pic-nics, and, in early spring, the yellow-gold sea of Nashville mustard in the lawn.

Overlooking Elmington is another synagogue, the Or-thodox shul, whose front doors have a good view of the tree dump. I've wondered if a teacher there has stood on the porch and stared at the piles, struck with the same peda-gogical fantasy: to convert a Christmas tree to Judaism.

Surely I am not the only person who wants to burn a bush in the name of text study. Yet when I searched for les-son plans or even a blog post, I found only crafts, and most of these featured colored tissue paper and battery-operated tea lights. No plan, Jewish or Christian, involved actual fire. Not even curriculum banks arranged by Torah portion. So I made one. My materials list featured "small conifer" and "box of matches."

And then I made my dream come true.

The goal was to make the Torah story more personal and memorable. Goal met. I did not mean for the rest of the school to think the building was on fire or to make our police officer hunt me down, but this happened, too.

But first I had to steal my second... small conifer. Please note that at no time, even when I asked permission from my director, at no time was this plant ever referred to as a Christmas tree. It was a bush. A *bush*.

I invited a special guest—Michael—to come to Izzy's grade and read the story of the burning bush in Hebrew and then paraphrase in English, and then I showed the bush scene from *Prince of Egypt*. We talked about how the bush was supposed to be weird so Moses would notice. We talked about "consumed," and how the fire was holy, not ordinary; and supernatural, not natural.

Then, to compare this with a natural, ordinary fire, we burned a bush.

My pitch-rich conifer burned so hot that the tree stand melted into a giant green macaroon, and so high that it looked more like the pillar of fire from a different Torah portion (B'Shallach). Michael took a photo of the kids' awestruck faces while they watched the bush burn and while, for once, they were speechless.

We learned that God would not have had much time to talk to Moses from an ordinary bush because ours was consumed in sixty seconds, and that the synagogue's air intake system can distribute smoke throughout the building within moments, thereby triggering widespread concern.

I said, "The bush is the pivotal point where Moses goes from loser to leader."

I said, "The bush is the vehicle by which God dictates the expectations Moses accepts."

But here's what Izzy said right now, when I asked what he remembered about our burning bush: "Well, we were outside on the porch and I remember everyone saying ohmy-gosh-*fire*-I'm-so-excited and then right before it happened we all fell silent. Then you struck the match and sent it up in flames and we watched it in silence. And in the middle some people started saying it was the coolest thing they'd ever seen."

"Awesome. Perfect."

"Wait, when was that?" he asked, sounding less certain.

"Three years ago."

"And we burned a Christmas tree, right?"

"No," I said, a little too loud. "We burned a *bush*."

Yesterday I stole another one for the brush pile. Nearly a month after Christmas, trees were still appearing at the drop-off. Metro brings the chipper truck every few days and a crew feeds it, tree by tree, to eat them all into mulch.

Radnor Lake accepts trees too. Their Trees for Trails

program chips trees on site while volunteers spread mulch on the paths. Weeks after there's always that little bit of tinsel aflicker along the lake.

Folks who bother to donate trees have much to teach our neighbors at Party House down the street. To rid themselves of their Christmas tree, Party Dudes simply drag it through their glass patio doors and toss it over the second-floor deck rail. I assume they assume the universe will make the tree go away. Their nine-foot Fraser fir has been on the curb for seventeen days so far, still wound with LED lights, still topped with a nice plaid bow, still thumb-screwed to a tree stand.

Neither the trash truck nor the chipper service is going to touch that. What justifies this level of entitlement? Who do they think they are? Who do they think is going to take this tree?

If it's still there on Friday: me.

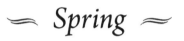

Spring

Quiet Point

Michael, Izzy, Beatrice, and I walk to Quiet Point at a quiet point of spring: when toothwort starts in earnest, false rue anemone is already a party, true rue anemone stands alone, and when spring beauty flickers low from nearly everywhere, peddling pink pollen and easy nectar.

Bloodroot white is gone, although the leaves—fleshy and veined—grow bigger and bigger, like ears of old men.

From leaf litter, which needs a better name than litter, other colors call: blue-white violets, violet violets, and sometimes the yellow kind. Sometimes the yellow is a fumitory flower, with its odd little tubes and flaring bells and odder name. And here are spears of trillium petals in the wine color that should be a somber note against whites and pastels but never is.

Elderberry leaflets line the path from the pawpaws, and we say we must come back to see summer blooms that make fall berries that make winter tonics that taste like cordial.

Pawpaws are still bare twigs with fuzzy buds, wine-dark, like the trillium.

Down the other side of Quiet Point is where any day now Dutchman's-breeches will froth the whole hollow above and below, so the trail curves brown and thin through what, when we squint, looks like snow.

Is Quiet Point quiet?

Not today, because on Saturdays families and joggers are up and down and up and down with "You have to go to the bathroom?" and "So I said to him" and "Postpone the meeting"; and here are headphones that leak playlists to the warm breeze; and here is that same air turbulent with after-shave; and here is a chattering quartet of ladies headed to the overlook even though the only green it looks over right now is invasive bush honeysuckle, which might not be as meditative a view as the ladies would like, but my guess is they consider the emerging leaves a thrill.

Here is the wrench of root when we yank honeysuckle, and here is the patter of soil when we shake a plucked stem, and here is the *shoosh* when we toss the bare-root bush to burn in the sun.

Here are train whistles, because we are only half a mile from the tracks. Here are barred owls asking *Who cooks for you, who cooks for you-all*? Here are we, talking twaddle at the patch of orange clay. We won't leave it until we've pried a piece from the trail to scribble terra-cotta on each other's wrists and spell "Izzy" on a fat root.

Here is wind through naked twig and branch, or through last year's whispering leaves on young beeches. Most trees at Quiet Point are leafless now and will be noisier next month, when they shade the white and violet and blue and pink and yellow and wine ephemerals back to sleep.

And here is the soft buzz of one bee—the first!—some

kind of little mining bee, drowsy, stumbling on the fossil-chunked hill; and who, in a way, is the not-so-quiet point of all this greening ground. Walkers are coming from both directions, so I hold a stick at his feet and he climbs on and I swivel to tuck the stick where boots won't smash. I am that lady who talks to sticks, but really I am talking to a bee who has just emerged from his slow nursery; has just punched his way out of a cocoon and out of the muddy plug his mom glued to the entrance of the hole last spring, right before she died. She laid girl eggs before the boys, from the back wall outward, and in a few days his sisters will emerge. It is his job to feast on nectar and pollen—pastels and wines—and to wait.

Here you go, darling, as I let the stick go. *Welcome to the spring.*

What White Tree
Is Blooming Now

It started. The procession of trees. The trees don't move, but the white does: white tree blossoms, from species to species. First, in late February and if not charred by sleet, come white flowers of star magnolia. Stinky Bradford pears are next, trees so ubiquitous in corporate landscapes—and invasive in natural ones—that when they froth white, even people who don't notice trees notice. Then dogwood. Everyone loves dogwood. Serviceberry, hawthorn, black cherry, yellowwood, black locust, and so on, week by week of the rolling spring, one white tree bloom after the other. It won't stop until summer, and by then, who is watching? By then, Nashville is a weedy jungle and we stay inside to escape the chiggers.

But I'll be watching. The procession is important. There are rules: only white, only trees, and only where I can see them while I go about my business. I call it the order of worship.

The order of worship sounds religious because it is, and I may sound religious but am not. The phrase was suggested by my favorite secular humanist Jew, and it hit the right chord in my Protestant past—of awe, ceremony, and gratitude.

Blossoms are both the object of wonder and the celebrants.

The order of worship is a framework to borrow. Structure keeps me sane when spring is crazy. A frame is an edge, a corner to grasp when the greens slide by too fast. Because spring doesn't turn on like a switch. It sneaks. *How long have the violets been blooming in the grass? Was this buttercup open yesterday?* Spring's first slow teases give hope that this year will be different, will be the year I can note every swell, give every bud burst its due, yet still keep my head. And then spring flies. Away. Erupts, more like. And suddenly I've lost my head and footing. I am under green water. My own backyard is foreign. The park trail where every bank was an old friend is a dark leafy tunnel and not an altogether friendly one.

But the order of worship helps. I can sort one category of miracle into place: white trees and when they bloom. I can compare progression from year to year. I can hold on.

Last Friday a few fat, fuzzy buds on the star magnolia split, froze, then rallied during the weekend's warmth so that today they've all burst into frenzies of their own snow. Even last night's wind only whipped off a few petals. To-morrow will find more on the pavement, and a hard freeze may burn them, but right now this moment is the star mag-nolia's turn.

Star magnolias aren't native trees and therefore do not function deep and wide in our habitat, but they are polite.

Educational too. Low suckers make good show-and-tell on urban nature walks, and buds are big enough for kindergarteners to dissect in the school lot. We poke nestled layers of petal, sniff the sweet lemon meant to lure pollinators. After bud burst, flowers are floppy, lank, like used tissue. But when viewed en masse, distributed on leafless twigs and especially on branches pruned for horizontal reach, they make exquisite tableaux. Even a trash alley is an ink wash painting if there's a star magnolia at the curb. It is the prelude tree in the order of worship.

Let me back up. The general, liturgical concept of order of worship has existed for thousands of years, but I first met it as the stated outline in the bulletins of a childhood church. The progression from prelude to postlude was fixed, ritualized. Signposts included the Apostles' Creed and the Lord's Prayer, the offering and doxology, scripture, sermon. Mercifully, it also included Mrs. Child's baked-fresh-that-morning white loaf as the Body of Christ. There has never been a tastier Jesus. But whatever the signposts and progression, the structure's function was to guide pew-bound congregants on a journey to deeper connection with a greater power.

White trees also follow an order. The progression depends on weather and climate and how biodiverse the viewing range—a few invasive thugs can spoil everything—and it unfolds because it unfolds, not because it is trying to lead us anywhere. Each tree does its own thing in its own time. The only deeper connection is the one between a tree's reproductive bits and a successful pollinator, because to re-produce is a tree's prime directive.

Frankly, the pious overtones of order of worship are put-ting me off right this minute. I could call the whole thing phenology and be done. Phenology is the study of key sea-sonal changes year to year. But where's the heft of history, the music of metaphor?

The order goes like this, but timing is fluid: star magno-lia, Bradford pear, serviceberry, American plum, flowering dogwood, hawthorns, rusty black haw, black cherry, black locust, yellowwood, oakleaf hydrangea, fringe tree, rough-leaf dogwood, southern magnolia, catalpa, persimmon, basswood, sourwood, farkleberry. (Farkleberry is my favor-ite to say aloud.) The order fattens or lengthens as I find new trees. Last year I had no idea that my kid's school had three serviceberries behind the teachers' lot. The year before that we found a yellowwood on a walk we'd taken hundreds of times.

The order is diverse. Some are native, some not, some are "desirable" landscape material, some not. Some are familiar specimen trees, some are tucked on hillsides off-trail in the woods. Some you don't notice until tiny flowers fall at your feet, some are in-your-face obvious, and some are smelled before seen.

Bradford pear blooms stink like dirty socks—and worse—but black locust blooms smell better than good. The first spring at our first grown-up house, I staggered through the backyard, face lifted, trying to breathe my way toward the source of something new: not honeysuckle vine, not star jasmine, but along those lines, and definitely with a hint of the Hawaiian White Ginger splash I bought from an Avon lady when I was twelve. Perfume ghosted every breeze and was especially haunting at twilight. Black locust, as I later learned it was, is sweet but deep, resonant, one of those creamy, heady florals no adjective can satisfy and that makes me want to press fistfuls of blooms to my face and swoon. I'd wake improved somehow, and with no chiggers despite full body contact with the lawn.

From inside a moving car on the interstate, black locust flowers are seen and not smelled. But if you walk your dog atop an overpass, you might get both. And if you know about the hole in the fence where the homeless man, the stoner kids, and the foxes have worn a packed path, you can squat below trees and pluck spent blooms from the grass. Most will be small bouquets nipped by squirrels, still sturdy enough to stand in a juice glass to perfume the house a few more days. Each flower is papilionaceous: butterfly-shaped and exquisite like other members of the bean family (sweet peas, redbud) and wet with nectar to call butterflies, ants, and bees. Black locust honey—also known as acacia honey—is said to be divine.

Bees lead me to another possible frame for the order of white. Beekeepers record the dates of nectar and pollen sources within a foraging area, and I've read that this can be called a floral calendar. Or the less poetic floral inventory. My so-called order of worship is a calendar and inventory too, but of my own foraging zone, restricted to color, trees, and my own fancies. When I ask my local bee friend about the floral calendar, she says that in real life bee-keepers simply talk about "what's blooming now." No need for a metaphoric framework. How practical. My version could likewise be "what white tree is blooming now."

I still vote for order of worship as the most useful term. It wins both despite the implied religiosity and because of it. This is the cultic language I reach for to describe the higher power that is a flower. As long as I don't get too literal assigning liturgical signposts to tree species, I can deal. My exception is for the prelude, because you have to start somewhere.

You have to finish somewhere too. At the bottom of every mimeographed church bulletin was the phrase "Worship ends, Service begins," which made no sense. Was it a recurring typo? Hadn't we survived the service, which was now, at last, ending? Later I understood that service could be verb as well as noun. The phrase implied that we had worshiped together, and we were now expected to go out and serve. Fine, but how do I serve my trees?

By trying to see them, learn about them, write about them. I'm afraid I'll come off as evangelical, heaven forbid, but I should invite others to see. I invite you to find your phenological order wherever your foraging range may be, whether it's a park or a parking lot, a driveway, a city block, or the interstate. To look around at "what's blooming now."

Our service is to deepen our connection to the place around us and to our place in it. This is greater power enough. And it can start with one bud on one tree, no matter the color.

Bring Back the Bones

At school pickup today the vice principal tapped at my car window. She bent down and told me gently, with troubled eyes, and twice because I didn't hear the first time and it sort of sounded like a question, "There is a dead bird under the car in front of you?"

At "bird," I realized I'd been hearing that word while children had chattered past my car. Pickup in the garage requires that all five grades—K through 4—file down this sidewalk to an assigned spot where they wait to be called. All five grades must have seen the bird. Fourth grade was still seeing it, because they were now sitting next to my hubcaps.

"Do you want me to get it?" I asked.

"What? No, no, I just…"

We exchanged several sentences that got me no closer to divining what it was she wanted from me. To not pop the bird with my tire? To wait for the car in front to leave so she could kick the corpse to the curb? To stay put until our security guard found a shovel? I had a migraine, so my brain had already taxed itself to remember which direction and how far to twist the car key to lower the window in the first place. But even on a good day I am not known for triumphs of interpersonal communication.

So I interrupted with, "I have a dog poop bag. You want me to get the bird? Let me get the bird."

"Really? Are you sure?"

"Sure, no problem."

And then, I was inspired. "I'll bring back the bones!" I said.

It was an English sparrow—they nest in the ceiling's acoustic fluffing every year—a male, dead but unmarked, and under the SUV's bumper but close enough to grab. I was wearing hand-me-down jeans that don't do well with bending, so I snatched the bird super fast, bag inside out, *whoosh.*

As I hustled back to the car, the vice principal said something like, "You are amazing!"

"I'm a volunteer naturalist!" I blurted.

"Really?"

"Really." And again, for some reason I said, "I'll bring back the bones."

While I slipped myself, my jeans, and the stiff poop bag into the car and tried to slow the throbs behind my left eyeball, the vice principal turned to face the fourth grade, which was collectively watching this drama. They were seated parallel to the row of waiting vehicles. They were bunched and staggered on risers as if in an amphitheater.

Panicked options began spooling. Bones? *Bones.* Could I impose myself on a biology lab's flesh-eating beetles? Pay a taxidermist? Find a fire ant mound? Pour a bleach bath and hope the skeleton didn't dissolve? Mummify in salt? Boil in a pot on the barbecue grill? Because there was already a backlog of tiny, well-labeled roadkill in my freezer. Because I haven't yet figured out the best way to get rid of soft tissue, and because all my dead things—all my would-be anatomy lessons—disappear from the yard no matter how carefully caged.

The sound of applause slapped me back to the pickup line. Fourth grade was staring at me, some smiling, some blank, but most were clapping. Over them stood the vice principal. She was egging them on, nodding, beaming, eyes bright with a Discrepant Event, a Teachable Moment, and so excited.

What I heard her say was this: "She is going to bring back the bones!"

I have not been clapped at in a long, long time.

But now I have to bring back the bones.

What a Robin Sees

I caught a robin redbreast red-handed. She was stealing soil from a tray on the porch. She took the seedlings too, but only to toss them aside. My lovingly planted seed tray had been repurposed as her own personal mud pile. Robins need wet soil to make their nests. Most yards nearby are solid turf grass with no soil in sight, but even my yard's bare patches aren't useful to her; they are compressed with our walking and cracked with no rain.

I sat on the porch to spy on the tray. She came, she stole, she flew across the street. Then I hid the tray under my chair. A moment later the robin was under my chair too.

After that I found a saucer to make a mud pile just for her. I put it where she'd first found the tray. She came, she stole, but my mud was too runny. It slipped and slopped from her beak. It reminded me of the Passover story where the Israelite slaves had to make bricks from mud with no straw.

I added real soil—not potting soil—and a handful of the random mess on the driveway: elm seeds, cedar needles, little chunks of bark, and short bits of dried grass. These gave the mud some bite, literally, and she could gather a big beakful each trip.

The trip is directly across our busy street to a hackberry tree, and the time between loads is about two minutes. When she returns, again and again, her breast feathers are muddy from where she's used her body to shape the bowl of the nest. That's when I check the birdbath I'd filled at dawn; it is now nearly empty and the color of chocolate milk.

So now I know exactly what it means when the birdbath is brown, and when my seedlings are gone: it is time to give a robin clean water and dirty straw.

Same Bat-Time

If our boy is tucked in and the sky is dry, I can ease outside ahead of the bats. They skate above the hackberries at dusk, replacing chimney swifts as if by agreement. After birds evaporate (where do they go?), two or three bats appear (where do they come from?). They loop, are joined by more bats—six, usually—and trawl lower, lower, louder; although loud is hardly the right word. Is there a term for "approaching audibility"? Through interstate roar, street noise, and heat-pump condensers, I listen for wing flaps and especially, miraculously, for the chatter—the faintest of quick clicks, like hamster nibbles from a cage in the next room. It's echolocation, as per grade-school science, and I can hear it.

"Only children and women under a certain age can hear the frequencies," said the bat biologist at the park program last fall, "and only three species in our area would be audible to the naked ear."

My naked ear is fifty years old. What is the "certain age" at which I go deaf to this new music? Why did I not know until now to walk outside and be still, to listen? Do other people listen? Will they listen to me if I tell them?

This must be how missionaries feel. I have good news, and it is urgent.

I had never even seen backyard bats until recently. For more than two decades my family was clueless to the existence of little brown (*Myotis lucifugus*) and big brown bats (*Eptesicus fuscus*) in our .22-acre plot. How is this possible?

In our defense, mosquitos are what flushed us indoors by dusk—Nashville has its fair share year-round. If the little browns had bagged a few hundred more a night, might we have lingered long enough to notice that we had flying mammals?

Big browns are beetle specialists. They eat the big beetles that thwack window screens of lighted rooms. On one of my first bat watches, I heard what sounded like hail hitting the metal roof of the porch every minute or so. The next morning I walked the roof to find the cause: May beetle corpses, with the middles missing. Is the belly of a May beetle the exact size of a big brown bite, or do bats only aim for the meaty part and ignore the ends? Sometimes on the driveway I find detached elytra, the crispy covers of beetle wings.

My two bat species adapt pretty well to human landscapes. Others aren't as lucky, but you might know this. You might already know bats are vulnerable to habitat loss, white-nose syndrome, pesticides, herbicides, fertilizers, turbines, artificial lighting, outdoor cats, and climate change, as well as to fearful folk like Aunt Bobbie who smacked a bat to death in her bedroom rather than let it exit the window it entered.

Before the sky blends to black, I see what I can't always

hear. So much flapping. I try not to compare them to Count von Count's bouncing bat buddies on *Sesame Street*, but I am helpless to this early memory. Bats can't glide like birds; they have to flap to stay up. The biomechanics of bat flight are too complex for me to understand, but I do know that when a bat dips it means dinner, because flight is interrupted when the tail membrane scoops an insect forward and up. It's an underhand softball lob but aimed at the pitcher's own mouth, and with a bug.

I'm grateful to see bats dip and rise, but bat noise is what I crave. Early spring is best: no window air conditioners, no insect song. Every year I wait for the first feeble crickets of spring, then summer's first cicada buzz saw and katydid chorus. I love those sounds, but now I hope for a delay, another night or two with a chance to hear bats. Any bat noise, call, or flap will do.

How many .22-acre lots in this suburban grid do these particular bats—these right now bats—scribe, sweep, simultaneously? Different yards but same bat time, same bat channel. Do my neighbors tune in? We protect what we love, but we can't love what we don't know, and we can't know what we don't notice.

Noticed or not, the six bats glean our sky and then loop above neighbors' trees: more hackberries, elm, ash, maple. Big browns can live up to nineteen years, which means the bats I see now could be the kids of parents I didn't see when we moved in.

But bats were here since before these fencerow trees, before the streetcar line, before the battle at the Rebel redoubt up the hill, before hunters found the salt lick by the Cumberland River, before people.

The last two robins are singing, but there are three, now four bats sharp against the sky. They circle, vanish, circle, vanish. A big one swooshes low over my head.

And then the screen door slams.

"Mom? Mom! Are you out here?" It's Izzy, who should be in bed.

"Here I am," I call from the dark. "Go in and get your glasses and come back quick because the bats are low!"

We stand together in the yard, our backs to the neighbor's floodlights, our arms touching.

"The sky is so beautiful," he says.

I point. "That bright star, see? It's Venus, over the streetlight."

"Where are the bats?"

The robins stop singing one by one. There are crickets, but far away. We hear a beetle buzz from the grass beside us, hear it rise in a wide and wobbly arc toward the pawpaw tree. And we wait.

Pop Quiz, Late April

Question: What is a "mushroom cup"?

1. The first and easiest cup in Nintendo's Mario Kart racing series

2. A college drinking game

3. What we found in the rain this morning under the sugar maple: an I-don't-know-the-species fungus (*Marasmus oreades*?), but for sure the fairy-ring type common in local lawns with a cap gone concave, its bowl tippling the cold rain all night and glinting now, still spattering, a wobbly goblet of flesh

Answer: All of the above.

Sycamore Currency

On American sycamore trees, buds are breaking. Under American sycamore trees, balls are breaking.

Seedballs stay on all winter, dangling from stems as tough as twine, but along about springtime they'll fret themselves free. And maybe before but definitely after, they will break. Spheres will soften and shiver into daggery tufts, into shards of seeds. Nutlets is the precise term for what, until breaking, had been huddled as a geometric collective, but seeds will do: pointy, hairy seeds the color of dead sycamore leaves. Seeds fall where wind and gravity say, but in such volume—by the bucketful—that they look like they don't want to be alone, as if they are homesick for tight-packed perfection. They accumulate in drifts along curb, sidewalk, storm drain. They become "sycamore snow."

It's hard to miss sycamore snow. But there was one secret stage of it even my husband and I had never seen.

First, have you held a sycamore ball in your palm? When it is fresh and tight, it may as well be a stone. But when ripe and soft, it may as well be a new state of matter. And this is when it must be squished, because to squish a sycamore seedball is a profoundly satisfying treat. One-handed is best, but two are fine. Underfoot is also an option. Even a thick-soled boot does not dilute the pleasure. There's a subtle give at first, like a shudder, and then, with the slightest pat, the whole thing surrenders.

After the surrender, and after you blow freed seeds to the wind, what's left in your palm is a hard little core. It's dull brown, the size of a blueberry, and wears shallow craters where the seeds had been.

Now for the secret part. Sometimes one whole sheet of seeds will pull away from the core and stay a sheet. The top doesn't change; it is the same curve of fluff. But underneath is mini-honeycomb as thin as paper. Empty of the core, it looks like the scalp side of a teeny tiny wig. And sometimes sunlight can glow through the honeycomb. It can blaze through the interstices from right there on the ground. This is what the dog showed us as we played fetch at the interstate easement.

How had I missed this step? Daily sycamores are all around: the Kroger parking lot, my morning red light at Vanderbilt. Twenty-First and Beechwood Avenues, and the parched row along the hellstrip on Magnolia Boulevard.

Perhaps I missed it because my daily sycamores are street trees. When street fruit falls, it lands on concrete and asphalt. But easement fruit has grass and rabbit holes and unclaimed dog poo to land on. Seeds are snugged against uneven soil that gets wet and dry, wet and dry, and they can shrug from tight spheres at leisure.

Cores, by the way, make great show-and-tell mysteries.

Only people who grew up near a sycamore can identify them. Even then, it's iffy.

Once I brought a shoebox of ripe sycamore balls to a second-grade party. I brought branches too, with balls still on the twigs. It was the yearly Christmas party we call a winter party because our K–12 school is legit diverse. And having already done classroom parties with my older child, and having witnessed the volume of fun foam, glitter, googly eyes, and acrylic felt purchased, pasted, and wasted at these parties, I signed up to create an activity that would be thematic but also not end up in the landfill.

The goal was to make winter gifts for birds: basic pine cone birdfeeders. Kids would select a pine cone, smear it with sunflower butter (no allergies, I checked), and wrap cotton string around one end and roll it in sunflower seeds. As a naturalist upgrade I added native tree fruit that kids might see locally, like hackberry drupes, sweetgum, catalpa pods, and sycamore balls. There were enough of the latter for every child to have two—one to break in class, one for later.

I rehearsed. I would bring my laminated bird poster and point to Nashville's winter visitors and residents. I would sing the white-throated sparrow song and the mourning dove song; I would mention how they and the dark-eyed junco like to stay on the ground but will eat seeds that fall from feeders. I would show the northern cardinal, the Carolina chickadee, and the tufted titmouse and say "They are probably in your backyard right this minute." I would use my teacher voice. And then all eighteen kids would go home and notice birds and grow up to be wildlife biologists and save the planet.

This was the plan. The reality is that these class parties with rotating activities destroy me. The model guarantees chaos: activity, craft, craft, snack at seven minute intervals, marked by a rotate-at-the-signal chime that no one ever hears. There was no time for bird posters, no time for context. Hours of prep were reduced to "Hi! Make this! Bye!" My screamed instructions were a whisper in the din. And of course, I had a migraine.

I think it is better to do a half-assed job than to do no job at all, so I keep trying. I am encouraged when kids get excited by common backyard detritus, like the girl who Zenned out massaging a spiky sweetgum ball between her palms. But when I'm presented with multiple kids who sit and stare at a piece of string and a pine cone as if they have no clue how to make the two items become one, or who are paralyzed with frustration when their first attempt fails, I am torn between an urge to smack them upside the head or slide them onto my lap and do the work for them. Neither action is sound pedagogical strategy.

But hey, at least children went home with biodegradable wildlife fodder instead of craft-foam glitter snowmen.

Overall the pine cone feeders were okay, but the kids were more stoked to keep as party favors their very own sweetgum capsule and an extra yet-to-be-smashed sycamore ball. I told them to wait for the smash until they got home, but no doubt there were snow flurries inside cars at pickup that day.

What I didn't realize at the time was that there is a humongous sycamore over the playground, which means these kids have regular unstructured access to leaves and twigs and seedballs. I'm glad I didn't know. I would have assumed every child had logged plenty of encounters with perfectly ripe sycamore balls, but I would have been wrong. Just because something is in your face all year doesn't mean you see it.

The point of my box of sycamore balls was to be sure everyone in that class knew what it felt like to squeeze a ripe seedball into buff-colored fluff.

What does it feel like? It feels like a flash of peace inside chaos. Like authorized demolition. Like a mini-ritual.

Another thing I learned was that Michael and I are not the only ones interested in the inner cores. Izzy tells us the bald little marbles are a thing on the playground. They are a commodity. He says most kids don't realize where they come from: "They just happen." But thanks to the tree over the wooden fort there are plenty of seedballs, and thanks to hundreds of stomping feet, cores are smashed free pretty quickly. And, thanks to K–4 imagination, these mysterious artifacts are regarded as objects of value. But the biggest surprise is what the kids call them: "Indian money."

What? When I was little, "Indian money" meant rocks, or if we'd known better, fossils: crinoid stems sorted from playground pea gravel. (If we'd known even better, we'd have said Native American or Indigenous Peoples instead of Indian.) Crinoid pieces look a bit like stone Cheerios but with ridges. They were traded as currency when I was in elementary school and thirty-five years later when our older child was too.

"They still are," said my fourth grader, "but so are the sycamore things."

A two-currency system!

Old school crinoids and new school tree trash!

I tried to imagine what kids bought on the playground. Was there a store? Did mean kids charge admission to the monkey bars? Or price the tire swing per ride? And I wondered aloud which Indian money is worth more, the crinoids or the cores?

"Neither," Izzy answered.

"Then what's the point?"

"To find them," he said, "and put them in your pocket."

True Nature

"Leaves-'n'-shit" is how Maggie describes my urban nature work. It's funny because it's true: look at my leaf collections, my Ziploc bags for seedy scat. She knows I know even city sidewalks yield endless observations.

On her spring visit she refused, again, to take walks with us. "Nature," she said, and winced. She wouldn't even get out of the car at the library, and when with my arms full of books I hollered, "Come see the redbud blooms," she barked her excuse from the window: "Wasps."

At seventeen she left Nashville for Manhattan, for the home she's found in city work, and where she'll stay except for a weekend a few times a year if we are lucky.

From the beginning we carried her, stroller-ed her, hiked her through the woods. She grew up blowing dandelions, chewing sour grass, sucking honeysuckle. When she was four and the cicadas came, she let them crawl up her arms. She cracked geodes with her dad, rescued worms from puddles. Ticks, chiggers, and mosquitos were no biggie, and she knew not to swat at bees. Or wasps.

At the park her favorite place was the old chestnut oak that fell off Mossy Ridge, her toddler, preschool, kindergarten, and grade school feet negotiating the wall of roots ripped perpendicular to the trail; her fingers excavating an infinity of puzzle pieces—shale and limestone—from silt and root branch. The wall was eight feet tall and more feet wide and as irresistible as a scab. She always called it "the city." When we asked why, she said that's where she worked.

If that wasn't virtuosic foreshadowing for our city girl, I don't know what is.

It's funny because it's true: I turn a city into leaves-'n'-shit; she turns leaves-'n'-shit into a city.

Samara

The photo showed maple seeds so big and gaudy I almost hated Michael for finding them without me. They wore wide wings with flowy ruffles like goldfish tails. And they were striped: the ruffles had ridges with sinuous veins of green and pink. What fancy maple could this be? A hybrid, an exotic ornamental?

I both love and hate when Michael texts me pictures from dog walks. I hate missing signs of spring but love when he doesn't, and when he shares. I hate the migraines that keep me home from even a twenty-minute circuit on sidewalks. Cars passing, dogs barking, sun at any angle are all prohibitive, as is sometimes the requirement to stand upright. The brain fog is not as big a deal because I need not remember left from right or which familiar street goes where; I just follow the dog.

Later that day I did follow the dog to the mystery tree. Michael and Izzy came too. There it was, by the curb of one of our usual routes. Don't you love when you see something for the first time even though you've seen it before?

It was a silver maple. An ordinary silver maple.

I thought I knew silvers. There are two I track through the year on our street. Their early bloom is the signal winter is done, and I watch the flowers turn from red to burnt orange before they morph into seeds. I break twigs to sniff the stink. I look for silver flashes when summer leaves flutter. And later, when leaves fall yellow and flat, before they vanish as curled cracklings, I'll collect a few. The bark I admire anytime.

And of course, I know the samaras: the winged seedpods. We take them home by the handful to toss from the top of the fort, because silver maples make the best helicopters.

The importance of maple helicopters cannot be overstressed. To twirl them is a must, like sucking honeysuckle or puffing dandelions or picking blackberries or weaving clover chains, or sneaking a handful of cleavers onto the back of whoever is standing next to you. These are seasonal pleasures and, if missed, take the world's slow year to come again.

One time at synagogue I led the kindergarteners on a nature walk. We needed leaves for crayon rubbings. But when we set out, we saw that the sugar maples in the front lawn had freed countless samaras throughout the parking lot, and from there we got no farther. Sugar seeds aren't nearly as big as silvers, but small helicopters are helicopters, and I watched until I had seen every kid gather and throw. I may have mentioned to them casually, once or twice, how maple helicopters work even better from a high place. So up the kids ran to the top of the stairs to fling samaras onto parked cars and heat pump condensers and me.

≈

At lunch today I asked Izzy and Michael why maple helicopters were important.

"They fly," Izzy answered. "They're cool."

Michael said, "The thing they were designed for by nature is what makes them so much fun to play with."

What nature designed is a single blade that generates lift as it rotates. The heavy seed drops, but the blade slices as it twirls, slowing the fall. They do fly. They are cool. I'd like to think they are universally fun to play with. I'd like to think everyone has twirled a maple seed at least once and would do so again should the opportunity present itself.

Michael added, "If you see a samara on the sidewalk, picking it up is better than not picking it up."

Although if you see a samara on the sidewalk, you probably see hundreds beside it. And though to some of us these are helicopters—or food, or seasonal markers, or handy examples of the same leading-edge vortices also present in the aerodynamics of bird, bat, and insect wings—to others these are the enemy. Lawn and Order have no lack of enemies. When lawn perfectionists complain about seeds hitting driveways and turf, they are missing the point. The point is that the world is working as it should.

In our own yard last year's sugar maple seeds—which stayed where they fell—will soon pop up as the usual crop of infant trees: countless babies of one little stem with twin seed leaves. How is this a problem? Spring's first lawnmower will simply slice them into food for the mother tree.

≈

Silver maple seedpods are the biggest of any maple, which is why they are the best (or worst, depending). I'm happy to know they can also come in stripes and pastels and goldfish tails. And, I forgot to say, they can be coated in silky down, a nearly invisible white velvet. Seeds often go through these decorative phases. It so happens the two trees I know best never do. On these, samaras drop green and empty as squirrels gorge; and weeks later, when squirrels find other food, samaras drop dry and full. By then, what lands on the sidewalk has matured to a color best described as manila folder.

Years ago, when those trees were new to me, a friend's cat died. My friend had called him her child. For some reason I thought an appropriate gift would be a little box lined with pink tissue and filled with five perfect, ripe silver maple samaras. The veins were exquisite, the blade margins whole and sharp. I left the box by her door. She never mentioned this offering and I felt stupid later, but at the time I imagined that the throwing of the biggest, most glorious helicopters could somehow help with grief.

The word "samara" means a dry winged fruit that is indehiscent, and indehiscent means it won't open without help. As in, help from squirrel teeth or my fingernail. Black walnuts are the most indehiscent thing I can think of—they never, ever open without help—although they are not samaras. Ash seeds are samaras, as are tulip poplar, hornbeam, elm. In Latin, samara means "elm seed."

The stripy samaras in Michael's photo were open. They'd been emptied, but with help.

Another name for maple samaras is keys. Because they look like keys. We stood under Michael's tree that day and saw fistfuls of keys at twig tips: full sets like janitor keys, and if they were real keys they would be so heavy they'd yank themselves out of any deadbolt. Along the street were dozens of key fobs that had already slipped, but not thanks to gravity; thanks to squirrels. Squirrels nip the twigs to better grasp a wad of keys in both hands, and to sit on a branch at leisure to extract from each plump pocket one wet green seed. And then they drop the empties.

What must this soft feast be to a squirrel who all winter has eaten only cached nuts and seeds dry, dry, dry and probably indehiscent as hell?

A fresh silver maple seed is the size, shape, and color of a soybean. Every year I nibble a few and wonder what I'm doing wrong. They are crazy bitter. And there's an awful astringency with a hint of unripe persimmon.

And yet maple seeds are famously edible. Especially silvers. Human foragers eat them roasted, parched, boiled, pickled, and raw.

I needed to try again. Between migraines I walked back to Michael's fancy tree to fetch a full samara. I pushed the seed out from the underside, bit it, spit it. Horrible. And then I looked closely at the fallen empties. The squirrels bite through the outer skin, but they bite through another layer I hadn't noticed. There is a white sheath of material between the samara pocket and the actual green seed. It's as if the seed wears a tight, white slipcover while it grows. Squirrels bite a slit through the outer cover and the slipcover and only eat the seed. So I made like a squirrel and did the same thing. And it was good.

I had been doing it wrong.

The slipcover is so bitter that it could be the bitter herb, or maror, at Passover. The importance of maror cannot be overstressed. Nor can the importance of Passover, and you can't have Passover without maror. It is meant to represent the bitterness of slavery and must be present on every ceremonial seder plate, and tasted (from a different plate) at crucial steps of the seder. Exactly which plant to use is subject to interpretation and local availability, but the most traditional is horseradish root, even though horseradish isn't so much bitter as hot. The root is so popular that you have to shop early to beat the other seder planners.

Wouldn't it be handy if a locally abundant herb could be maror? And even better if it was legitimately, uncomfortably, memorably bitter? And if it didn't cost eight bucks a portion? And if all we had to do to get it is walk to the nearest silver maple? The timing is perfect; samaras start showing up on Nashville's sidewalks the same time Nashville's Jews start prepping for Passover.

I'd like to share one more samara vignette. I've been sitting on it for years, not sure what to do. I sent one version to an editor but was reprimanded. She told me an essay should not merely convey awareness of racism but must also subvert racism. Of course we must subvert racism. But what if awareness of racism *is* the story? What if there is no subversion to report? Is such a story not worth telling?

I've put it here because it is about maple seeds but also about presumption and mistakes and a memorable bitterness. If I gave it a title, which I won't, it would be this: "Another White Lady Says Something about a Black Lady's Name."

Here:

One bright July day a young woman came to the door selling magazine subscriptions. I never trust sellers or the sponsoring companies, because the first is taking advantage of me and the second is taking advantage of the first, but the name printed in all caps on her lanyard was Samara. Samara! My skin was far, far paler than hers and I hesitated—I didn't want to look like I assumed anything other than we were two women alone on my porch. I couldn't dare ask if she knew what her own name meant, and besides, maybe there were fifty other meanings for Samara I'd never heard of. But no way in hell was I buying anything, and of course I had a migraine, so I panicked.

What I should have said was no thank you. What I said was, "Were you named after the tree seeds?"

Our sugar maple hangs over the porch, and I showed her the helicopters and explained, "These are samaras. Aren't they wonderful?"

And god help us both, I tossed one in the air to demonstrate the twirl.

Catalpa Verbs

While we all wait for our boys, talk drifts to Pilates, interior designers, vacations, hair. I have nothing to say.

What I do have, above our watched soccer field, are parking lot oaks with baby galls like translucent green bubbles. I have black walnut trees behind us, with old shells underfoot ready to throw. I have red cedars green by the sideline, who puff pollen if the month and breeze are right. At the pre-K fields I have the white oak, which is a couple hundred years old, at least. But I do not have the social skills to add these topics to a conversation. My fear, again, is that my enthusiasms are eccentric and beyond sharing.

But when catalpa trees flower, I go ahead and blurt. I take action.

Catalpa blooms. It sure does. Catalpa blooms such blooms. Big, frilly, and so exotic I'd never buy them if they were in a flower shop, which they aren't, and if I bought cut flowers, which I don't. They look like some made-up tropical thing on a sunscreen bottle, but catalpa is a native tree. They are as Nashville as Osage orange or black locust, and nearly as redneck as a hackberry.

Catalpa leaves. Catalpa leaves are cartoon hearts preposterously huge. One heart I patted today was longer than my elbow to fingertip, and that's without the stem.

But what leaves the biggest impression are the flowers. They froth in bouquets of up to thirty white two-inch funnels with scalloped tiers, with flecks and stripes of burnt orange, yellow, and purple.

Catalpa seeds. Those tiers and colors are for bees, not us. I don't know how the arrangement translates to ultraviolet, but where we see gaudy spatters bees see runway lines that scream "enter here." And when the bee enters a tube for advertised nectar, maybe its bumbling back scrapes pollen from anthers in the ceiling. And when the bee bumps the next blossom at the next tree, maybe a grain of the earlier pollen sticks to the stigma and slides to the ovary. And as white frills shrink, the ovary magically stretches into a crazy twenty-one-inch bean pod to dangle on a twig all winter and burst with hundreds and hundreds of paper seeds next spring.

Congratulations! Cigars all around.

Indian cigar tree is another name for catalpa. And lady cigar tree.

Some people take Indian cigar literally. A YouTube slideshow documents one man's attempt to smoke catalpa three ways: the whole pod lit at one end, a wad of seeds plugged into a "peace pipe," and seeds "in a bong with ice." His earnestness inspired me to transcribe his results as a found poem. The concluding slide:

I think
that the nickname for the tree was coined
just because of the appearance of the dried beans resembling
    cigars.
No Native American
in their right mind
would smoke them
in any form.

Catalpa smells. Standing at a tree today, I rip a blossom to find a wet collar. It smells like syrup and jasmine. I lick. Sweet. Is the fragrance in the wet alone or does it thread throughout? The leaves wear extrafloral nectaries all summer, but are nectaries stitched in flower fabric as well?

A bee's sense of smell is a hundred times more sensitive than ours. To a bee, what is it like to rootle inside a catalpa bloom? Is the perfume bliss? Agony? Just another day at the office?

Smell is one clue to tell a northern catalpa (*Catalpa speciosa*) from a southern one (*C. bignonioides*). The two are so similar it's hardly worth the trouble to key them apart, but just so you know, southern leaves stink when crushed. Like faint skunk yet not completely unappealing.

Catalpa worms. In summer it's time to look for something else that grows on catalpas: fish bait. The tree is host plant for the catalpa sphinx moth. The female lays her eggs only on catalpa, and when babies hatch they only eat catalpa. Catalpa worms, they're called, though technically they are caterpillars. I haven't met one yet, but I see why they make famous bait. They cost nothing and require no digging; they literally grow on trees. They are meaty, long enough to divvy into thirds, and tough enough to stay on a hook even when turned inside out, which is the optimum presentation. Optimum for the fish, not the caterpillar.

Another name for catalpa is fish bait tree. And worm tree.

Here's a neat connection to the leaf nectaries: because nectar seeps from nodes in the leaves all summer, the sweetness attracts ants, and ants can keep caterpillar numbers in check. Catalpa worms can defoliate a mature tree. Ant and tree help each other.

Catalpa roots. I don't go into detail when I mention these trees to friends and acquaintances. It's too much, even without worms on fishhooks. But I can't stop mentioning catalpa. The flowers need to be seen and smelled because they are magnificent—an intense pleasure for an intensely short time—and they are part of where we are. They root us. They take their turn in a progression of tree blooms that cue every stage of early spring to fall, whether we pay attention or not.

So I may casually recommend this or that nearby or on-the-way-to-work tree where, at the very least, blooms may be admired from the car, if not, as I would like to suggest, admired by pressing one's face into a pyramid of blossom.

And then, last Sunday, I got a text from a fellow soccer mom: "Just thought I'd let you know I think of you every time I see a catalpa tree. They are lovely. Happy Mother's Day. Hope you had a perfect one."

And thanks in part to her, I did.

Grandiflora Gesture

Magnolias are blooming. Nashville has several species: some evergreen, some not; some native, some not; some with small leaves, some with clown-shoe leaves; and even one secret magnolia, the Tennessee state tree—tulip poplar—in the magnolia family but quiet-like, on the downlow. But the magnolia I'm talking about is the southern magnolia, the one you think of when you hear the word "magnolia," the one that from April to September blooms creamy flowers the size of soup plates, flowers that turn you more southern—for better or worse—every time you ID the fragrance from afar. *Magnolia grandiflora*.

Actually this southern icon is more southern than Nashville, where it is an adventive species, brought here by people unable to resist a lawn ornament so stately and green, and who had enough lawn for a tree that gets up to eighty feet high and forty feet wide. There is no shortage of them in town—even, improbably, along sidewalks—and there are dwarf cultivars for humbler lawns and tighter spaces.

In spring we usually smell southern magnolias before we see them, which is as it should be. An ordinary breath should be interrupted by that first-of-year slap of extraordinary, of sugared citrus, soft when far away but sharp up close. Sink your face into one low flower. Sniff to be sure you can handle it, then breathe, snuffle, snort, huff the lemon from bowl to brain.

Bees go nuts looking for nectar (there is little), taking pollen (there is plenty), dislodging anthers, and bruising petals. Have you ever touched a magnolia flower and learned, too late, that one hasty poke, one accidental crease bleeds a caramel scar? Even an unblemished bloom doesn't last long. Cream soaks to the color of milky tea, then droops, drops.

After college a friend of mine cut a fresh magnolia blossom, padded it with tissue and bubble wrap, and mailed it to a man she thought should love her more. Later she realized the flower would not have ended the journey in the same condition as it began, and might even have arrived a uniform brown, or worse, a cross-hatched khaki.

There's a surprising amount of brown on a southern magnolia in spring. When newest leaves are coming, oldest leaves are going, and they detach and drop one slow leaf at a time. They are thick, big, brittle. Stand near a tall tree on a hot May day and listen for the clatter.

While you're there, look for patterns on the waxed upper side of a dead leaf. Shiny spots, rings, concentric circles— they look like water damage on good furniture, but lovely. Turn the leaf over to see the shade side and to pet it, because it is rust-colored velveteen.

Another magnolia marvel to look for, but not until September, is grenades. After bees and beetles do their job, a flower's center swells into a cone of bright red seeds, each cone about the size of a hand grenade, each seed about the size of a soybean. Cones pile up under trees and beg to be taken home. Why take home? The better to pull seeds at your leisure. Why pull seeds? Because of the marvelous, mesmerizing, elastic thread that keeps a seed in place until you pull it.

"Ectoplasm" is what my husband calls the string—uncanny, otherworldly—but the texture reminds me of Silly Putty or that slime kids make in science class out of glue and borax. Funiculus is the botanical name, and if you know the old song "Funiculi, Funicula" about the Funicular cable railway up Vesuvius, you know these words are about things that hang by rope.

Pull a red seed from its pocket to see how far the rope can stretch. Pinch straight out, don't rush—three inches, four, more? Pull to see how thin a thread can get before it snaps, both ends curling into nothing. Pull as slow as nerves can bear, and it may well be a contemplative practice.

My friend who mailed the magnolia bloom never heard back from her man. We wondered if he thought she'd UPS-ed a dead flower as a botanical breakup note or whether he was just a jerk. But what I wonder is if he opened the box and found her perfect white, fragrant, ambrosial blossom so lovingly swaddled that he simply panicked and ran. Too *grand*, her *flora*, for a small-hearted boy who did not deserve the gesture.

House Wren

On a bird hike last spring, our group of just-met walkers stared at an eastern bluebird atop his box. This is the beginning of the walk, when I hope I can pass for sociable.

I mention to the man beside me, "All my bluebird houses are stuffed with house wren nests. Tiny twigs from floor to roof."

"Ah," he drawls, "the house wren."

"Yeah, that song gets on my nerves. It drives me nuts."

"Charming bird," he monotones, clipping the "g" because he is old Nashville and I mean old. "Charming song."

After that I am as silent as the sticks in my bluebird box.

A house wren is tiny, adorable—nearly as cartoony cute as the Carolina wren but plainer and slimmer. The Carolina's song is infinitely variable, whereas the house wren's is infinitely the same. The *Audubon Field Guide* is not wrong to describe the house wren's song as "gurgling, bubbling, exuberant... first rising then falling." The Cornell Lab of Ornithology says "effervescent," "rush-and-jumble." All true. The melody is sweet until you hear it all damn day, every damn day, so that you wonder if you are being tormented with a hidden recording on autoloop. The sequence is mechanical, downright diabolical in monotony, and it varies only in directional source: from which bluebird box it sings.

A male house wren is a real estate bully. He claims all cavities and he stages them the same way and for the same reason: to impress a potential mate. Each box is plugged floor to hole with twigs and only twigs—no moss, no cedar bark, no grass, no leaves. Meanwhile, when Carolinas or chickadees or titmice or bluebirds house hunt, there is no room. The early bird got the house—all the houses.

Every spring I make several trips around the yard each day to clear out all but one house, hoping to keep the properties on the market for other species. But even if this works, it may not be safe for other birds to settle so close to house wrens. They are known to give neighbors the boot, and destroy eggs and kill nestlings. Of course, other species do this too. Right now, starlings are evicting my red-bellied woodpeckers from their own fresh cavity in the sugar maple. Birds look out for number one. It isn't "charming," but it makes sense.

The lazier way to free up houses is to wait until the house wren's scheme works and a mate accepts. Then I can excavate rejected boxes in time for late broods of chickadees or titmice.

But the song. I can do nothing about the song. My heart drops to my ankles when I hear it the first time each spring. It's an earworm. Well, no, it isn't. A worm insinuates, and the house wren song is too short to insinuate as a background chorus. True earworms can shift to the fore mid-verse, but the house wren's song is more direct, a burst of descant about three seconds long that defies phonetic transcription. Let's say: *Scrit-scrit-scrit-tsak-tsak-tsak-triiiiiiiill-tskeet-tee-tee-tee-tee-tee-oh*. Descants are ornaments to a foil of proper melody, but this ornament is a solo. It's a frippery fillip of a gewgaw, like a decorative lozenge on a picture frame but without the picture or the frame. And it happens nine to eleven times a minute.

Scrit-scrit-scrit-tsak-tsak-tsak-triiiiiiiill-tskeet-tee-tee-tee-tee-tee-oh.

None of my local birding friends is vexed by the house wren song. The internet doesn't seem to mind either. I suspect my problem is my own. Have you heard of misophonia, or selective sound sensitivity syndrome, or "When Annoying Noises Send You into a Rage"? The most common trigger cited by people with this condition is the sound of other people chewing. Amen to that: I max the stove fan during family dinners for the white noise. On a related and worse note, I once failed a graduate exam because the man next to me hocked phlegm so often that my brain forgot everything except to count seconds between expectorations (the average was nine). Another low point: running to the neighbor's privacy fence in the wee hours and bruising my fists on the pickets while screaming "Stop it, stop, shut the hell up!" because this neighbor, who seemed never to be home, left her two large vocal dogs outside, where they barked. All. Night. Long.

Scrit-scrit-scrit-tsak-tsak-tsak-triiiiiiiill-tskeet-tee-tee-tee-tee-tee-oh.

Now I can add house wren to the list. The song is a selective sound to which I am so sensitive that my subconscious mind might flit, once or twice, maybe, to the Red Ryder BB gun in the attic. Just a fantasy, I swear, and never to be revealed on a bird hike. My conscious mind, meanwhile, is so loath to harm even the smallest of creatures that it moves me to transfer trapped insects outside. Not only ladybugs—the biting, swarming, exotic, multicolored lady beetles—but even brown marmorated stink bugs, the most hated exotic agricultural pest in the state. I rescue assassin bugs from the shower. I angle a stick in the water barrel as a ramp to dry land. I catch wasps in Tupperware to toss out the window. I live trap our basement mice.

So if this tenderhearted naturalist suddenly fantasizes about murdering a wren, something is wrong.

What's wrong is the song. Nothing muffles it. Not my other neighbor's 24/7 window air-conditioning unit, and not our new double-glazed windows.

Scrit-scrit-scrit-tsak-tsak-tsak-triiiiiiiill-tskeet-tee-tee-tee-tee-tee-oh.

Scrit-scrit-scrit-tsak-tsak-tsak-triiiiiiiill-tskeet-tee-tee-tee-tee-tee-oh, ad infinitum.

Mercifully all this mishegas is for a limited time. The song starts with spring migration and ends when the wren either fails or succeeds. Last year no female acquiesced, so he split. The year before that he disappeared after the final brood. And then, peace.

The peace leaves me time to reflect. And to admit that for a few weeks every spring I am an asshole.

As soon as the trigger is gone, so is my trigger finger. I

can go back to relocating carpenter bees and reburying grubs. I can hang laundry unrushed. I can read in the hammock. I can be sane.

This spring I said I'd be ready. As soon as my heart dropped to my ankles the first time, I would permit the singer to keep one home staged, but I would not clear other boxes more than once a day. I would limit my time in the backyard. I would attend to work inside my own house. I might even finish painting the bathroom I prepped and primed ten years ago.

I'm the human, so it is my job to look out for all of us, not just number one.

And then this happened:

It was the second day of May, prime time for new things to see and hear and smell and do, but I was missing all of them, because to see and hear and smell and do would hurt. I was propped in bed with a migraine, listening to audiobooks at low volume and wearing a turban stuffed with ice.

"There's a bird trapped in the porch!" came Michael's yell from the kitchen.

I knew it was a house wren.

And it was a house wren.

I crept outside to prop the screen door open so the wren could find a way out. But then I thought I'd hurry things along, because this was the kind of migraine that screamed to get back to a dark bed. And, not thinking rationally, I clapped so the bird would fly. The bird flew. Not out the open door but into the screen above. *Bang.* And then back toward me, into another screen. *Bang.* And so on. *Bang,*

bang. And then the bird was belly-up on the concrete floor and did not move.

Oh no, oh *no*.

Still not thinking clearly, I reached for my bee rescue net, a fine mesh on a bamboo pole, and laid it over the body so I could ease a stiff placemat underneath and transfer the mat outside where the bird could recover.

There I was, kneeling in dirt by the shed, in sweaty pj's and a poofy ice hat, holding a paralyzed songbird tangled upside down in a blue net. The wren was hopelessly snared. This is why birdbanders use netting to catch birds—it works—and why I should have used anything but.

"Fetch me some scissors," I barked.

Michael jogged inside and came back to slap a pair in my outstretched hand as if I were a surgeon whose eyes could not safely leave the patient. My eyes were fixed on the wren's eye. It kept blinking, black and wet, rimmed with the sweetest edge of alternating dark and pale, dark and pale, as if someone dotted a circle on white paper with a fine-tip pen.

I cut the net carefully with the big blades, terrified I would snip a toe, fighting flashbacks of trimming a newborn's fingernails for the first time. The bird lay there on the placemat blinking, legs up, one foot now wearing a slipper of sky blue mesh I could not cut away.

"If you need me to," Michael offered, "I'll hit it with a rock."

This was meant as a kindness, for me and for the bird.

The placemat was an illustrated alphabet chart Maggie

and Izzy had eaten from as tots. As I sat there minute after minute, as I guarded the bird from neighborhood cats and the Cooper's hawk and the red-tailed hawk and the crows and every possible predator I suddenly sensed was slavering from the periphery, as I waited for the bird to recover its wits, I sort of lost mine, because I found myself wishing the bird was paralyzed closer to the letter H on the placemat: H for house. Or to the W, for wren. But, alas, it was positioned somewhere between. The body was an example that did not stand for anything, illustrate anything, teach anything. It was random.

"The wildlife rehabbers are in Joelton and I can't drive a car today," I babbled. "Maybe it'll survive in a shoebox until tomorrow? I don't know if this is a male or female. They look alike to me. What if she's got eggs? What if she's got babies? What if it's a he, and he is my enemy? Oh, Michael, this is the bird I wanted to shoot through the eye!"

"I know."

"But I didn't mean it!"

"I know."

And Michael patted my hair, knowing everything. He stood behind me under the noonday sun and stroked the dirty hair below my ice hat, a caress I did not deserve because I am the asshole who talks about shooting a native songbird through the eye. And it was my fault the wren was trapped in our porch in the first place. I had not sewn up last year's rip in the screen (soccer ball) or this year's rip (baseball), and wrens are small and acrobatic and inquisitive enough to slip through slits in screened walls. And then I was the one who tried to herd it, and instead, I hurt it.

"Let's turn it over," Michael suggested.

"That won't work."

More minutes passed. Michael went inside, came back out. The blinking continued. We stared at the blue foot. We stared at the sweet, rounded breast-belly combo pointing up at the sky, and saw it panting, panting, up, down so fast. Would shock kill it? The sun was bright. The placemat was shiny.

"Jo, let's turn it over."

Like Michael knows anything about birds. He's never stared at a feeder or read about birds or watched a birdbanding or talked to a birder or taken a single bird hike in his life.

But waiting wasn't working.

So I found a pair of gloves and knelt again on the ground. I eased one finger between the blue foot and the good foot, and at that very moment the bird's toes grabbed me and used my finger to pull up and push over and fly free. The wren shot low across our yard and through the next. We ran to check if we could see it, to watch if it landed okay, if maybe it was pecking at the blue, but it was gone.

The rest of that day I kept the windows open, hoping to hear a house wren.

Nothing.

I still don't know if our blue-slippered bird was male or female. After the migraine eased and I was able to read pages and screens again, I learned that to the casual eye, there is no difference between house wren sexes but size, and when only one bird is paralyzed on an alphabet placemat there is no basis for comparison.

I'd like to think he was a he, and that his body really was an example—that it did stand for something, illustrate something, teach something—and was not random.

I'd like to think he was my enemy and that my guilt has made him my friend.

The next morning I heard it: *Scrit-scrit-scrit-tsak-tsak-tsak-triiiiiiiill-tskeet-tee-tee-tee-tee-tee-oh.*

And my heart, instead of falling, flew.

Guided

When you prep all morning for the guided hike and leave home in plenty of time. When you hit Interstate 40 and realize your phone is in the kitchen. When you turn around to get it, then change your mind and turn around again, then regret that and turn around a third time but not at the kind of exit where it is easy to do so. When you burst into the kitchen and surprise your family and grab your phone and start again but are now hopelessly late. When you enter the Cedars of Lebanon driveway as a white government van leaves but do not trust your instincts to follow it. When you jog to the lodge to ask where the field trip went and no one knows. When you drive where you think the van went (based on the vague description in the flyer) and you drive and drive and drive down a dark gravel service road with brown puddles bigger than your car and perhaps too deep for your axles. When you lie on your back under the car to fish a three-foot stick from the chassis. When every gap in the forest is a cedar glade, but every cedar glade has been destroyed by off-road vehicles. When the map says the gravel will end at a junction with a paved road—which you will take no matter where it goes—but it dead-ends twenty feet before that, at a stack of boulders, a mound of Japanese honeysuckle, some beer cans, and what looks like a grave: two white wooden crosses wearing plastic poppies the color of blood.

When you stop rehearsing what you will say when you meet up with the van.

When you turn the car around and slide sideways through the same brown potholes. This hike in what the Department of Agriculture calls "the largest contiguous cedar glade-barren complex in public ownership in middle Tennessee" has been on your calendar for a year. You wore earrings.

When you start looking at those gaps in the forest.

When the sun disappears and the sky shortens and rain taps through the window. You like it. Your husband knows where you are because, of course, you have a phone. And it's the wrong time of year for hunters and the wrong time of day for hell-raisers, so you do it: you get out and get wet in a ruined glade in the moment, this moment, the only one you have, and hear field sparrows, hear a pewee, hear wind in the cedars, and smell more honeysuckle. You are not expected on that hike. You are not expected anywhere. You remember you are lucky to be alive. The rain stops. You like this too.

When you search what's left of the nearest glade and instead of habitat see hundreds of shotgun shells in turquoise, blue, green, red, and for some reason want them all. When you have leisure to note the contents of illegal campfires: beer bottles, clay targets, shoeboxes, particle board from cheap shelves. When yellow star grass blooms from the crest of a tire track. When you load a Ziploc with brass rifle casings because no one can ask you why. When you pee without hiding in the woods. When you spot three shotgun shells lounged in a clear puddle and they are a still life, though the water moves.

When you get back to the gravel and drive from flower to flower you suddenly see in the unmown verge—leaving the car running, turning it off, it doesn't matter, no one's coming—and you kick through poison ivy to kneel at green milkweed mobbed with milkweed bugs and at shooting stars twined with crossvine and you poke the pale nodding heads of false gromwell and steal one little bloom of heal-all and you rub the red ribs of Gattinger's prairie clover so you can breathe the spice from your fingers. When you remember oxeye daisies are on the state invasive list but wonder, who in the world can't love a daisy? When the lyreleaf sage turns out to be eastern white beardtongue and isn't it amazing how sometimes redbud leaves are glossy red hearts before they grow to green? And when hot-pink rose verbena lures you so close you see the darling lavender spikes of vervain and the pouting blue lips of Gattinger's lobelia and while you are still squatting you find your old favorite, glade sandwort, and you can understand why people call it wild baby's breath, but the name still sounds funny, as if it is the babies that are wild.

When the rocks are made of fossils, and the moss is made of stars.

When the one prickly pear left standing is in the lee of

an uprooted cedar, a former giant of a tree that pulls you closer and, if you're careful of the cactus, could make a good place to sit. The wood has worn to the same dull silver as the limestone of the glades, but it is smooth under your sliding hand, under a now cloudless sky.

When you hope the shitty road that was too long coming in will be longer going out, and with no one on it to tell you what, or how, or why, or when.

Coda

Nature Lessons

You are not obligated to complete the work
[of repairing the world], but neither are you
free to desist from it.

Pirkei Avot, 2:21

Once upon a time, bugs were bad. All moths ate clothes. All caterpillars ate all plants. All birds ate seeds. And the nearest nature was a Metro Park twenty minutes away by car.

Then I joined the Tennessee Naturalist Program.

One watershed moment in the course came early, on a hike led by Margie Hunter, an award-winning conservation educator, author of *Gardening with the Native Plants of Tennessee: The Spirit of Place*, and a creator of our curriculum. When she paused next to a plant, she kept using the word "function," as in how that plant functioned in its community. Function? Community? Suddenly native plants were not just a pretty choice, or a culturally historic choice, or even a choice; they were a necessity. Native plants are the producers with the deepest and widest function in their ecosystem. Because plants and animals evolve together in a

place—in every place—they develop specialized relation-
ships with each other for which there is no substitute.

The famous example for "specialized" is a monarch butterfly. Monarchs can't lay eggs on any plant but milkweed,
because that's the only plant the caterpillars can eat. No
milkweed, no monarchs. Meanwhile milkweed doesn't
want to get eaten, so it protects itself with toxins; but monarch caterpillars, who also don't want to get eaten, have
evolved not only to survive the toxins but also to use them
as protection against predators. They even have a clever way
to eat the leaves, so the sticky "milk" in milkweed doesn't
glue their mouths shut.

Specialization is not the exception; it's the rule. "Ninety
percent of the insects that eat plants can develop and reproduce only on the plants with which they share an evolution-
ary history," says entomologist Doug Tallamy, who wrote
the game changer *Nature's Best Hope: A New Approach to
Conservation That Starts in Your Yard*. Spoiler alert: nature's
best hope is us. If we add plants native to where we are—
even if we start with one plant in a pot on a porch—we help
restore habitat where we are. Our entire food web depends
on insects and other invertebrates, "the little things that run
the world."

We've run out of time to plant only for decoration.

Every state has official naturalist programs, and most are
organized into three parts: classwork, fieldwork, and volunteer work. The goal is to build a corps of volunteers who

can help local habitat in limitless ways. They can lead field trips, teach kids, run workshops, talk to garden clubs, pull invasives, count butterflies, write articles, support legislation, track phenology, input data, restore a grassland, adopt a stream, plant trees.

Imagine if there was a volunteer naturalist on the boards of companies who develop property, manage property, sell property. Imagine a naturalist at every lawn care franchise and pest control company; in every city and state government; and at hospitals, prisons, and schools. We need naturalists at conventional plant nurseries too, where natives, if present, are usually a few cultivars shoved in a corner.

Aside from certification programs, there are oodles of ways to learn about native habitat. Local parks and conservation groups offer free events year-round, like guided walks, workshops, community science projects, and volunteer opportunities, all staffed by friendly folk eager to share nearby nature. Nashville's Metro Park naturalists are stellar at this.

You can also teach yourself. Go outside, pay attention. Go again tomorrow, and the next day, every day.

"Stay curious," urged nature writer Ellen Meloy. "Know where you are—your biological address. Get to know your neighbors—plants, creatures, who lives there, who died there, who is blessed, cursed, what is absent or in danger or in need of your help. Pay attention to the weather, to what breaks your heart, to what lifts your heart. Write it down."

≈

Nature needs our help. Habitat loss is why more than one-quarter of all birds have disappeared in the past fifty years and the reason one-third of all plant and animal species could go extinct in the next fifty. Those two words, "habitat loss," are how I summarize and simplify the countless complex threats to the health of our planet, from global warming to microplastics. If I tried to address each threat one by one I'd be paralyzed by ecological despair. So, I figure, if the world is losing habitat everywhere, then I have the power to add habitat somewhere.

Our yards and neighborhoods are now critical habitat. If more people believe this, maybe we can tweak standard practices to be more sustainable. We need fewer pesticides, herbicides, fertilizers. Fewer all-night security lights and automatic sprinklers. Less concrete. More green space. Bird-safe windows. Many, many more native plants—especially the keystone producers—to host insects, feed birds, and keep us all alive.

We can do this work as play, with family, friends, and neighbors, with free seeds and plants shared by local gardeners, and with guidance from organizations that show us how: the National Wildlife Federation, Audubon Society, Xerces Society, Wild Ones, and other leading voices. Like Doug Tallamy's Homegrown National Park, they encourage "small actions by many people" to make big changes in biodiversity. What we start at home—on the balcony, in the yard, by the sidewalk—can grow into networks of beautiful, functional communities where humans and the rest of nature thrive together. The only way we will solve anything is together.

But the first step, as always, is to look around.

Credits and Acknowledgments

This is the bit where I'm to thank everyone but can't, so a part will need to stand for the whole. Even a little collection of essays demands a big accounting of people in whose debt I remain.

Michael, Maggie, and Izzy: you are the bedrock beneath the Ordovician, the sky above the chimney swifts. Thanks for putting up with caterpillars in the kitchen, with sudden inattention on foot or in the car ("Meadow!" "June bugs!" "Cooper's hawk!"), and with the loss of our yard to wild creatures, which means Beatrice must be taken elsewhere to play. Thank you, Jean Brichetto, for wanting to print out everything I've written, and for being ready for adventure, even though I'm usually in bed. To Dr. Ryda D. Rose, my favorite "academician": I hope you are pleased I finally made a book, and with a university press, no less. Thank you, Taunia Rice, for reading my stories, and for a lifetime in company with your "particular and peculiar" talents, love notes in the mailbox, and bouquets on the porch.

Thank you to Marguerite Avery for picking my manuscript from the pile, and to Emily Jerman Schuster for combing through it with a sharp eye and a kind heart (and a taste for redbud blooms). I am grateful to the team at Trinity University Press, especially Steffanie Mortis Stevens, Sarah Nawrocki, Burgin Eaves Streetman, and Bridget McGregor.

Margaret Renkl, thank you for your kind offers of cross-pollination, both literal and literary, and for the lesson that promoting one's own work can help to promote the work of others. Most of all, thank you for leading your readers, story by story, to a fundamental shift in the way we think about nature. Janisse Ray, thank you for the candid and caring phone call exactly when I needed it, and for sharing book world advice. And to writers Nancy Lawson, Margo Farnsworth, Ann Shayne, Catherine Caffey, and Michael Sims, I am grateful for your emails and texts of support.

Because of various, regrettable character traits, I hardly told a soul I was putting a book together. So when I thank this next lot, it's for friendship and support in general. No one but me is responsible for any errors in the essays.

I am indebted to my first naturalist teachers in town: Kim Bailey, Deb Beazley, Sandy Bivens, Rachel Carter, Heather Gallagher, and Vera Roberts, all either past or present at Warner Park Nature Center. What a thrill to keep learning from and with you.

Since completing the Tennessee Naturalist Program, I can thank Richard Hitt for years of nerdy emails and the kind of hikes that take an hour to go five feet; and Gail Eichelberger for sharing "Clay and Limestone" in more ways than one, and for reminders to look at the sky. Patty

Ghertner, you are a joy to work with on game-changing "generative dialogues." Thank you, Margie Hunter, for backyard digressions, catching the fox, and texting whenever a great horned owl asks if we are awake too.

At the University School of Nashville, thank you to Lisa Preston, lower school naturalist teacher, for being my let's-make-the-campus-an-arboretum buddy; to Cynthia Lee, who created the program; and to current naturalist teacher Lauren Hagen, for letting me help with plants and plans. For saying yes to caterpillars in the classroom and butterflies out the window, I am forever grateful to master teacher Heather Webber. Thank you to the Green Roof crew, including Oscar, Esha, Nell, Emilia, Ivy, Annie, and Clara, for asking if I'd like to help with native habitat and then listening to the ongoing answer.

Maureen May, thank you for your Second Sunday Gardeners, and for the most hospitable yard in town. I am grateful to all the Second Sunday members who share their time, seeds, plants, passion (and passion vine), and even caterpillars, as well as their goals to grow habitat, food, and friendship.

For helping me branch toward neighborhood service, thank you to my Metro Beautification and Environment commissioner, Miriam Mims; to Julie Berbiglia, education specialist, Metro Water Services; to Cayce McAlister, whose brilliant idea planted Weed Wrangle; and to the soil mates from Wild Ones, especially Richard Hitt, Patty Ghertner, and Diane Scher.

At Centennial Park, thank you to Lauren Bufferd, direc-

tor of the Parthenon museum, for loving the park's hackberry trees; to Denise Weyer, superintendent of natural
resources and nature centers, for listening to my dream to
protect Nashville mustard; to Judy Wright for asking me to
share Parthenon sidewalk nature with the Herb Society of
Nashville; and to my Sportsplex kibitzer, Mary Comfort
Stevens, for wanting wild violets.

Thank you to cedar glade champions Kim Sadler, Jason
Allen, Milo Pyne, Sunny Fleming, and Roger McCoy.
Thorunn McCoy, thanks for chats in the hallway by the
lockers.

Todah rabah to Julie Greenberg for the invitation to look
at Micah's nature, and to Sharon Paz for letting me take students outside and to burn a bush.

Thank you, Tony Gonzalez, for suggesting I might have
something to say at WPLN, and for showing pictures of
your family's butterflies and bees. For kind invitations to
embarrass myself for something I love, I am grateful to
Magnolia McKay with WPLN's *This Is Nashville*, Caroline
Eggers with Nashville Public Radio, Mark Fraley with the
Mark Fraley Podcast, and Greta Requierme with *Volunteer
Gardener*.

Thank you to my first friends—Allison, Krissie, Nancy,
and Dawn—and to Brenda, Laurie, Kenneth, Sam, and Tim
for the kind of kinship that picks up where we leave off, no
matter how many years stand between. Thank you to Maria
and Jan for sister love and wanting to make butterflies.

I am honored to be even a tiny part of several groups who
do good work, like the Middle Tennessee Chapter of Wild

Ones, ReWild Nashville, the Hillsboro–West End Neighborhood Association, Second Sunday Gardeners, Bird Safe Nashville, the Tennessee Native Plant Society, and the Tennessee Naturalist Program. Thank you to Monika Pretz and Bryn Beauchamp of the Tennessee Environmental Council for letting me help with urban meadows; to Meg Morgan at Root Nashville for tree talk; to Debbie Sykes of the Nashville Wildlife Conservation Center for insights into creature care; to Vicki Turner at the Nashville Tree Foundation for celebrating big, old trees; to Bethany Crandell for scheming with me about habitat; and to Lynn Green for asking me to write for the Nashville Tree Conservation Corps.

Speaking of writing, thank you to Roseanne Spain, Jan Slough, and Susan Owen for being sterling teachers in grades five, six, and twelve. You each asked for my first book, and here it is, only forty-odd (and forty odd) years later than I hoped.

But over all and under all, I come back to Michael, Maggie, and Izzy. This book is for you.

Place-based education: These essays were written from Bigby Cannon limestone on the Bosley Springs tributary of the Richland Creek watershed of the Middle Cumberland River in Nashville; in the Central Basin of Tennessee; in the "ancestral hunting and traditional Lands of the Cherokee, Shawnee, Choctaw, Chickasaw, and Creek peoples"; in the Mississippi Flyway.

Versions of these essays were originally published in the following publications, and I am grateful to the editors of each: "Hummingbird Winter," December 2023, in *Short Reads*; "Guided," 2022, in *Ecotone*; "This Is How a Robin Drinks," January 2020, in *Brevity*; "What White Tree Is Blooming Now," 2018, and "Dragonfly, Secondhand," 2020, in the *Hopper*; "Same Bat-Time," 2020, in *Stonecrop Review*; "Field Trip Leavings," 2016, and "What a Butterfly Means," 2019, in the *Fourth River*; "House Wren," fall 2019, in *Fourth Genre*; "Can't Eat Just One," June 2018, in *City Creatures*; "Raptor-Ready," winter 2018, in *Longleaf Review*; "Eponymous," 2018, in *About Place Journal*; "It Was a Yellow-Billed Cuckoo," October 2018, in the *Common*; "Winter Solstice," December 2018, in *Chapter 16*; "Bring Back the Bones," 2018, in *Flyway Journal of Writing and Environment*; "Naked Ladies and Cicadas," May 2017, in *Hippocampus*; "Animal, Vegetable, Mineral," 2017, in *Vine Leaves Literary Journal*; "A Dandelion Is to Blow," 2016, in *storySouth*; "Walking Onions," fall 2016, in *November Bees*; and "Sidewalk Fig," 2021, "Leaf Prints," 2015, and "What a Robin Sees" 2023, in SidewalkNature.com.

Joanna Brichetto is a certified Tennessee naturalist and writes the urban nature blog *Sidewalk Nature: Everyday Wonders in Everyday Habitat Loss*. Her essays have appeared in *Brevity, Short Reads, Ecotone, Creative Nonfiction, Fourth Genre, Hippocampus,* the *Hopper, Flyway,* and the *Fourth River*. She lives in Nashville.

Printed in the USA
CPSIA information can be obtained
at www.ICGtesting.com
JSHW021811120924
69690JS00005B/7

9 781595 342997